Security Blurs

Security Blurs makes an important contribution to anthropological work on security. It introduces the notion of "security blurs" to analyse manifestations of security that are visible and identifiable, yet constructed and made up of a myriad and overlapping set of actors, roles, motivations, values, practices, ideas, materialities and power dynamics in their inception and performance. The chapters address the entanglements and overlaps between a variety of state and non-state security providers, from the police and the military to vigilantes, community organisations and private security companies. The contributors offer rich ethnographic studies of everyday security practices across a range of cultural contexts and reveal the impact on the lives of ordinary citizens. This book presents a new anthropological approach to security by explicitly addressing the overlap and entanglement of the practices and discourses of state and non-state security providers, and the associated forms of cooperation and conflict that permit an analysis of these actors' activities as increasingly "blurred".

Tessa Diphoorn is Assistant Professor in the Department of Cultural Anthropology at Utrecht University, The Netherlands.

Erella Grassiani is Assistant Professor in the Department of Anthropology at the University of Amsterdam, The Netherlands.

Routledge Studies in Anthropology

www.routledge.com/Routledge-Studies-in-Anthropology/book-series/
SE0724

Security Blurs
The Politics of Plural Security Provision

**Edited by Tessa Diphoorn
and Erella Grassiani**

LONDON AND NEW YORK

First published 2019
by Routledge
2 Park Square, Milton Park, Abingdon, Oxon OX14 4RN

and by Routledge
52 Vanderbilt Avenue, New York, NY 10017

Routledge is an imprint of the Taylor & Francis Group, an informa business

British Library Cataloguing-in-Publication Data
A catalogue record for this book is available from the British Library

Library of Congress Cataloging-in-Publication Data
A catalog record for this book has been requested

ISBN: 978-0-8153-5676-9 (hbk)
ISBN: 978-1-351-12738-7 (ebk)

Typeset in Sabon
by Apex CoVantage, LLC

Contents

vi *Contents*

Illustrations

Figures

Table

Contributors

Laurens Bakker is Assistant Professor at the Department of Anthropology at the University of Amsterdam, The Netherlands. His research and publications focus on land law and land conflict in Southeast Asia, as well as on the influence of informal militias in local politics, societies and economies. He is presently principal researcher for the "Securing the Local" research programme, which comparatively researched the role of non-state security actors in Indonesia, Kenya and Nigeria.

Lars Buur is Associate Professor at the Department of Social Sciences and Business at Roskilde University, Denmark. He is the coordinator of the research programme "Hierarchies of Rights: Land and Investment in Africa" and has published widely on vigilantism, sovereignty and state formation in South Africa and the recognition of traditional leaders and ruling elite formation in Mozambique.

Tessa Diphoorn is Assistant Professor at the Department of Cultural Anthropology at Utrecht University, The Netherlands. Her research focuses on everyday security and policing, and she is currently conducting research on police reform in Nairobi, Kenya. She is the author of *Twilight Policing: Private Security and Violence in Urban South Africa* (2016).

Erella Grassiani is Assistant Professor in the Department of Anthropology at the University of Amsterdam, The Netherlands. Her current research is part of a wider project on privatisation and globalisation of security and her research traces the flows of (Israeli) security worldwide and looks at the way cultural ideas, technologies and consultants move around globally. In the past she has done extensive research on the Israeli military. She is the author of *Soldiering under Occupation: Processes of Numbing among Israeli Soldiers in the Al-Aqsa Intifada* (2013).

Rivke Jaffe is Professor of Cities, Politics and Culture at the University of Amsterdam, The Netherlands. Working across the boundaries of anthropology, geography and cultural studies, her research focuses primarily on intersections of the urban and the political, and specifically on the spatialisation and materialisation of power, difference and inequality within cities. Her current work studies public-private security assemblages and the associated transformations of governance and citizenship. Her publications include *Concrete Jungles: Urban Pollution and the Politics of Difference in the Caribbean* (2016) and *Introducing Urban Anthropology* (with Anouk de Koning, 2016).

Line Jakobsen is a PhD candidate at the Danish Institute for International Studies and the Department of Social Sciences and Business at Roskilde University, Denmark. She is currently doing research on security practices and political subjectivities in and around large-scale coal mining in Colombia. Her master's thesis on community policing in Bolivia, which included four months of fieldwork in La Paz, received the prize for the best thesis of the year of the university department.

Helene Maria Kyed is a social anthropologist and currently the head of a research unit at the Danish Institute for International Studies. She has done research on policing, justice provision and post-conflict state formation in Mozambique (since 2002), Swaziland (since 2010) and Myanmar (since 2014), particularly exploring authority, sovereignty and violence in urban as well as rural contexts. Her latest edited book is *Policing and the Politics of Order-Making* (2015).

Erika Robb Larkins is Associate Professor of Anthropology and Sociology and Director of the J. Keith Behner and Catherine M. Stiefel Program on Brazil at San Diego State University, USA. She received her doctorate in Cultural Anthropology from the University of Wisconsin, Madison and also holds an M.A. in Latin American Studies from the University of Chicago. Her research and teaching focus on violence and inequality in urban settings. Her first book, *The Spectacular Favela: Violence in Modern Brazil* (2015), explores the political economy of spectacular violence in one of Rio's most famous favelas. She is presently working on her second book examining the private security industry in Brazil.

Perle Møhl is an anthropologist and filmmaker, specialising in visual and sensory anthropology, everyday communication and pragmatic semiotics. She has carried out fieldwork in rural France and French Amazonia and has published two books based on this fieldwork, as well as a series of films, namely *Village Voices: Coexistence and Communication in a Rural Community in Central France* and *Omens and Effect: Divergent Perspectives on Emerillon Time, Space and Existence*. Her research on biometric technologies and vision in connection with border control is based at the University of Copenhagen, Denmark.

Moritz Schuberth completed his PhD in Peace Studies at the University of Bradford, UK. His research focuses on non-state armed groups, peacekeeping, security governance and urban violence. He is the author of recent articles in *Africa Spectrum*; the *Journal of Eastern African Studies*; *Conflict,*

Security & Development; the *Journal of Peacebuilding and Development*; *Contemporary Security Policy*; *Stability: International Journal of Security and Development*; *International Peacekeeping*; and *Environment and Urbanization*. He currently works as Monitoring, Evaluation and Research Manager for the global humanitarian agency Mercy Corps in the eastern Democratic Republic of the Congo.

Atreyee Sen is Associate Professor in the Department of Anthropology at the University of Copenhagen, Denmark. She is a political anthropologist of urban South Asia. Her research and publication trajectory focuses on large-scale militant political movements in the city that create micro-cultures of violence in confined urban spaces. She is the author of *Shiv Sena Women: Violence and Communalism in a Bombay Slum* (2007) and co-editor (with Dr David Pratten) of *Global Vigilantes: New Perspectives on Justice and Violence* (2008).

Jeremy Siegman is a political anthropologist and Lecturer on Social Studies at Harvard University, USA. His research uses ethnography and social and political theory to explore questions of settler colonialism, the market and contemporary politics in Israel/Palestine. His book manuscript in progress is entitled *Enemies in the Aisles: The Politics of Market Encounter on Israel's Settler Frontier*.

Acknowledgements

The idea for this volume was born out of the two panels that we organised with Rivke Jaffe at the American Anthropological Association (AAA) in Denver, 2015. The two panels were titled "Security at Large: Governance and Citizenship Beyond the State" and focused on the exploration of the pluralisation and hybridisation of security. We would first like to thank all of the contributors to these panels for setting the groundwork of this volume: Lars Buur, Daniel Goldstein, Beatrice Jauregui, Erika Robb Larkins, Dennis Rodgers, Atreyee Sen, Jeffrey Sluka, and Finn Stepputat. From these panels, and particularly the discussions we had afterwards, the idea of this volume emerged and throughout the journey, we have been fortunate to have other contributors whose ideas matched the ethos of this volume join this endeavour. Jeremy Siegman, Laurens Bakker, Perle Møhl, Moritz Schuberth, Line Jakobsen, and Helene Maria Kyed: we would like to thank you all for coming on board to this project and providing insightful contributions.

In addition to the authors, we fore mostly want to thank Rivke Jaffe, a dear colleague and friend, who brought us together through the ERC SECURCIT project at the University of Amsterdam. Her idea for this large research project not only brought us together, both as colleagues and friends, but it has shaped a lot of our thinking about security, and we will be forever grateful for this. We are therefore also extremely pleased that Rivke was willing to contribute to this volume with an afterword. We would further like to thank Erika Robb Larkins, who has been indispensable through her willingness to write a wonderful foreword to introduce this volume. We also thank Dennis Rodgers for the brainstorming session in his office in Amsterdam, which formed the building blocks of this volume. In addition, we are grateful to Barak Kalir and Nikkie Wiegink for their insightful comments on the introductory chapter. We would also like to thank the team at Routledge, especially Katherine Ong and Marc Stratton, for their great assistance and leadership in making this volume possible.

And last, but not least, we thank Aksel and Niv for giving us some working time in Nairobi to really get to the conceptual heart of *Security Blurs*.

Tessa Diphoorn and Erella Grassiani

Research funding

This work draws on research funded by the European Research Council (ERC) under the European Union's Horizon 2020 research and innovation program (grant agreement no. 337974, SECURCIT).

Foreword

Erika Robb Larkins

State Police. Civilian Police. Private Security Guards. Community Police Officers. Neighbourhood Watch. Civil Defence Groups. Military Contractors.
Soldiers. Urban Security Patrols. Vigilantes. There is no doubt that security
has become a critical, ever-present part of everyday lived experience across
the globe. Moreover, in many places, lived experience is shaped by the overlapping presence of multiple security actors, configured in oftentimes confusing and imprecise relationships with one another. This collection of articles
reckons with this empirical reality by asking what such muddy, ambiguous
forms of security provision can teach us about the workings of power, governance, inequality, sovereignty and citizenship. With contributions that are
theoretically expansive and demonstrate a nuanced understanding of the
local settings in which security is performed, each author in the volume inter-
rogates the blurring of security in a different way.

While the interdisciplinary literature on security has long noted pluralisation as a central theme, fine-grained examinations of the ways in which different security actors interact with one another have been absent. Scholars
have instead focused attention on one particular species of security worker,
like "the police" or "the military". Such choices, no doubt, are often the
consequence of practical limitations, but it is clear that most security personnel are part of larger security constellations that merit urgent exploration.
The articles in this volume do just that. Importantly, they eschew clear lines
between providers. This focus directs attention instead to grey areas of productive convergence where we can better understand how security is structured and performed, as well as its effects on those it is intended to secure.

Each of the pieces departs from a focus on a "security blur" to examine
the convergent relationships of individual security actors with various kinds
of security others. For example, public and private border agents negotiate
their work with the non-human actor of ABC (Automated Border Control)
software in the Copenhagen Airport. A supermarket in an Israeli settlement is a site for juxtaposition of a seemingly friendly, commercial security
placed within an overall climate of militarisation. Vigilante justice coexists
with everyday forms of community security provision in the Bolivian city, as
boundaries between actors are constantly negotiated. The work of Civilian

and State police officers is at once entangled and structured by power hierarchies in Maputo, Mozambique. Competing actions of local tough guys,
police and politicised societal organisations shape the daily experience of
citizens in Jakarta. A diverse set of security providers in urban Haiti is
simultaneously the provider and creator of insecurity. And citizen-vigilantes
engage in politicised forms of moral policing in Mumbai.

Across a great diversity of settings, the pieces in this volume focus on
structural and performative features of security. Security blurs in the structural realm stem from a general kind of fuzziness about whose job it is
to provide effective security to the population, to which part of the population, and for what motives and with which purposes. In almost all of
the cases presented here, we find that not only is security not the exclusive
purview of state-led actors, but that what is provided by the state looks
different depending on a range of factors, such as social class and location
in urban space. Thus, with state-led security being implemented unevenly
across global, national and city borders, fissures are shored up by myriad
actors (including non-human ones) who both compete and collaborate with
state actors. It is exactly these contradictory assemblages that are well captured and analysed by the ethnographies presented here.

Security blurs, like all forms of security, are also actively performed. Performances are key to staking territory and to delineating borders. They
often incorporate material culture such as cars, weapons and clothing. The
pieces in this volume also take up issues of scale and space in a provocative
way, tracing performances from the realm of the body to city to nation to
globe. And while the blur itself is often a productive force (one that enables
expansion of security regimes in ways that empower certain providers and
disempower others), it too has limits. These limits are often expressed
through performances that work to curtail the overlap between groups,
such as when private security guards are prohibited from wearing uniforms
that look too much like the police. The limits of "acceptable" performance
indicate that the blur itself is in constant negotiation, and that its boundaries are just as revealing as are the murky spaces between different groups.

Finally, in reading these essays, we should ask: what are the effects of
security blurs on those groups that are the most vulnerable to insecurity
and exploitation by security actors? In many cases, security blurs flirt with
illegality – as actors abuse the authority of their positions for personal gain,
benefitting from the impunity that comes from being authorised to uphold
(or break) the law. Blurring means that citizens sometimes cannot tell *who*
they are dealing with. Motivations are obscured; the political backers of
certain security providers may be distinct from those who citizens see and
interact with. And while all security is inherently political, we might ask if
there is something especially political about the blurs described here because
they often work to conceal larger power structures. This helps us to see how
citizens – in whose name security is often enacted – are at worst victimised,
or at best disempowered, by slippage in roles of security personnel.

In short, these ethnographically grounded pieces address important questions about the nature and consequences of security blurs, suggesting that that security is, perhaps, better understood as the sum of its parts. This book will be an important reference for interdisciplinary readers interested in how security and insecurity intersect with issues of power and governance. Furthermore, the volume highlights precisely why the ethnographic approach to studying security is so crucial, as it is only through the kind of careful and patient portraits of local life presented here that the entanglements of such a pluralised security world can be understood.

Introducing *Security Blurs*

Erella Grassiani and Tessa Diphoorn

In my neighbourhood[1] in Southern Tel Aviv, white cars can be seen patrolling the streets, with blue and yellow markings, looking very much like regular Israeli police cars. I have learnt to distinguish them, though, by their yellow and blue lights, as opposed to the blue and white lights of a "real" national police vehicle. The neighbourhood is known for its poverty, crime, prostitution and, more recently, for the many African refugees who have found shelter in the small houses around the market. The city of Tel Aviv has neglected this "backyard" of its shiny sea front. In reaction to the increasingly "dangerous" situation in this neighbourhood and others like it, the municipality has initiated a combined "Urban Security Patrol" (Sayeret L'Bitachon Ironi or SELA): security cars belonging to the municipality are staffed with municipality security personnel and police officers. Both actors wear similar dark uniforms with comparable emblems on their arms, and often both are armed and carry handcuffs and other security equipment. According to the official site of the municipality, the units are formed to prevent criminality and terror acts, to aid the police in securing the city and its citizens and to protect the city's property.[2]

* * *

This illustration of a specific type of security provision in the first author's everyday life is comprised of what we shall call different *security blurs*: performances aimed at providing a sense of (perceived) safety that includes numerous and different actors, roles, objects and aesthetical appearances that overlap, and through this overlapping, create various forms of blurriness. Such occurrences raise questions about what security is, who is providing it, whom it is provided for, and how it can be interpreted by the actors involved. In this case from South Tel Aviv, we could examine the relationship between the different actors – the municipality security personnel and the police officers – and their motivations and goals during these patrols, or we could focus on the materialities and aesthetics, such as their uniforms and vehicles, in order to uncover and understand what type of security we are observing. More importantly, we could question what such performances of security teach us about sovereignty, power and the legitimacy of actors in the eyes of the public and of themselves? What social problems can such multi-faceted patrols encounter and produce? What political dynamics are at play that define how such security work targets specific neighbourhoods and populations?

In this volume, we want to explore such questions in order to better make sense of the various security acts and performances observed across the globe that are based on an intermixing of actors, objects, goals and roles, and through this intermixing, create new and different ideas and interpretations of what security is, or can be. We propose to do so by introducing the concept of *security blurs* and showing the complexities that are overlooked when focussing on isolated actors and their activities alone. The idea of "blurs" is often used to indicate ways of obscuring, of producing uncertain and unclear phenomena. Rather, we use it here to show how within security acts (as defined emically by many of the relevant actors), there is a multitude of interrelated dimensions and meanings that are intertwined. Firstly, we use "blurs" as a noun, to refer to the visible and identifiable manifestations of security that constitute multiple, overlapping set of actors, roles, motivations, values, materialities and power dynamics in their inception and performance. Secondly, we use "blurs" as a verb, to refer to the performative and effective characteristic of security performances, namely that through its enactment, a performance of security itself changes and with that our understanding of it. Security blurs are thus identifiable phenomena, like the patrol in Tel Aviv, but also have an effect that blurs our interpretations and understandings of power and social order.

By advancing the concept of security blurs, we aim to present a new anthropological approach to security by explicitly addressing the overlap and entanglement of the practices and discourses of state and non-state security providers, and the associated forms of cooperation and conflict that permit an analysis of these actors' activities as increasingly "blurred". These blurs and the way they come into being are deeply political, with the state/non-state boundary negotiated, crossed and defended according to the underlying interests of the actors involved. The past couple of decades have seen a proliferation of anthropological research on policing, which discusses the range of security providers that include formal state institutions, such as the police and the military, but also non-state actors such as gangs, community policing organisations, vigilante organisations and private security companies. Furthermore, this body of work has highlighted the pluralisation and hybridisation of security provision (Albrecht 2016; Albrecht and Kyed 2015; Colona and Jaffe 2016; Diphoorn 2016; Diphoorn and Kyed 2016), thereby demonstrating that policing and security are inherently relational and processual. Yet, at the same, most of the studies tend to zoom in on the daily security practices of one of these actors as the prime focus of analysis. This edited volume makes an important new contribution to anthropological work on security by going beyond previous research that considers security actors in (relative) isolation and by specifically engaging with the ways in which practices, ideas and objects are entangled and result in diverse forms of blurring.

Thus, this volume focuses on the indistinct boundaries that characterise the entire spectrum of security providers as it aims to understand how such boundaries and their blurring are inherently political processes and concern issues of sovereignty and power. By doing so, we seek to problematise the use of dichotomies such as "formal" versus "informal", "state" versus "non-state", and "illegal" versus "legal" in our understanding of security. Negotiations over cooperation between different security providers – whether this will occur, and if so how and to what end – and the security act itself always involve (competing) claims of authority and control. Understanding the diverse meanings of such political processes requires detailed ethnographic studies of everyday security practices across a range of cultural and national contexts, which this volume aims to provide.

By focusing on the blur itself, i.e. the point at which blurring comes to the fore and is visible, and on the process of blurring to understand its effects, this volume concentrates on the power struggles and uncertainties that emerge from these entanglements and overlaps between security providers. Drawing on different cases from across the world, this collective work demonstrates how blurriness between security actors and practices involves contestations that (re)produce ambiguities for ordinary citizens and for security actors themselves. Security blurs emerge when different actors interact, thereby reconfiguring security ideas, logics and practices. However, security blurs should not be equated with instances of collaboration or competition; rather, we should understand the negotiation of boundaries – state/non-state, formal/informal, human/non-human and corporate/voluntary – as central to political practice. By elaborating this approach, and by focusing on the everyday encounters through which new understandings and enactments of security develop, this volume provides a novel and critical analysis of security realities across the globe and moves beyond existing concepts such as pluralisation.

Each contribution in this volume explicitly takes a "security blur" as the starting point of its analysis and shows how they come into being by exploring how and why the entanglement between different security actors, materialities or responsibilities occurs in a specific context, and what larger politics this reflects. In the opening chapter, Jeremy Siegman focuses on military/civilian blurring and how security blurs emerge in Super-Israel, a supermarket in an Israeli settlement in the Israeli-occupied West Bank. In the following chapter, Moritz Schuberth analyses the multiplicity of armed groups in Haiti and shows how security blurs emerge in the process of labelling such actors. Also focusing on the assortment of various local security providers, Laurens Bakker investigates the blurs that arise when *ormas* (societal organisations) provide informal security activities within their communities in Indonesia. In the fourth chapter that takes us to Mumbai, Atreyee Sen analyses how security blurs emerge through militant moral policing practices that are simultaneously performed by a range of actors (low-ranked policemen, security guards, and lower class female civilians) and are shaped by notions of morality, violence, religion and sovereignty. Claims to sovereignty also lie at the heart of Helene Maria Kyed's chapter on Maputo. Kyed analyses the entanglements between civilian and state policing and how both policing actors and police practices produce security blurs. Also focusing on community practices, Line Jakobsen and Lars Buur's chapter on La Paz portrays the entanglements between community policing and vigilante-like practices that result in "blurred (in)securities". And in the last chapter on the Copenhagen airport, Perle Møhl describes the continuous blurring of responsibilities, decision-making and ongoing negotiations between the various human actors, and between human and non-human ones in the process of determining risks.

This volume thus comprises diverse case studies that approach security blurs from different perspectives, even as they all draw on rich, in-depth ethnographic fieldwork. And through this data, they are able to: 1) unravel the complex processes of boundary manipulation and negotiation in relation to national, territorial and economic interests, 2) address the ambiguities of security and uncover the power struggles that lie at the core of processes of blurring and 3) demonstrate how blurs impact the daily lives of ordinary citizens. By unpacking both the similarities and disparities across different cultural, political and geographical contexts, this volume addresses the globally urgent topic of security, demonstrating the range of security performances and their centrality to political contestation.

After a brief discussion of the anthropological focus on security, we will show how we use the concept of "security blurs" through a three-dimensional approach and how these dimensions are discussed throughout the various chapters. We end with a note on the key role that ethnographic fieldwork – a core component of an anthropological approach – plays in identifying and unravelling security blurs.

Anthropology of security

Anthropologists have engaged with issues that could be categorised as security and insecurity for a long time, yet only in the last few decades has the idea of an "anthropology of security" emerged as a potential focus within the discipline whereby security is regarded as "a critical object of study in its own right" (Glück and Low 2017, 283). In a useful overview, Limor Samimian-Darash and Meg Stalcup (2016) divide the existing scholarly work into four main fields. The first focuses on "violence and state terror" and primarily includes work conducted in the 1990s and 2000s that dealt with both urban insecurity and armed conflict (see Feldman 1991; Nordstrom and Robben 1995; Scheper-Hughes and Bourgois 2004; Caldeira 2000; Low 2013). These studies show the complexity of violence and its structural and everyday nature. They mostly take the individual as focus point and hence overlook the collectivity of feelings of (in) security. The second field consists of works on "military, militarisation, and militarism", where a new focus was found in perpetrators and the organisational aspects of state induced violence. Most studies focused on the military (Ben-Ari 1998; Grassiani 2013; Winslow 1997) and more recently, on state police forces (Denyer Willis 2015; Fassin 2013, 2017; Garriot 2013; Jauregui 2016; Karpiak 2010).

The third field includes work on "para-state securitisation" and security produced "outside" the state, for example, by gangs (Jensen 2008; Rodgers 2006; Van Stapele 2015), vigilante organisations (Bakker 2015; Buur 2006; Pratten and Sen 2007), community policing initiatives (Kyed 2009; Ruteere and Pommerolle 2003), and private security companies (Diphoorn 2016; Grassiani and Volinz 2016; Larkins 2017; Mynster Christensen 2017; Higate and Utas 2017). The influential work by Goldstein (2010) also belongs to this field, in which he calls for a critical anthropology of security and encourages researchers to further reveal the "multiple ways in which security is configured and deployed – not only by states and authorised speakers but by communities, groups and individuals – in their engagements with other local actors and with arms of the state itself" (2010, 492). In line with Goldstein's call, a growing body of work has come into existence, including edited volumes (Maguire et al. 2014; Pedersen and Holbraad 2013; Hurtado and Ercolani 2013) and several special issues in journals such as *Etnofoor* (2015), *Conflict and Society* (2017), *Qualitative Sociology* (2017) and *Anthropological Theory* (2017). In this last issue, Zoltán Glück and Setha Low (2017) introduce a sociospatial framework for the anthropology of security. This framework includes looking at how security is produced through various forces and how "*security operates as a productive process*" (281, italics in original) on its own. With this framework, the authors claim that we can better understand the contradictions and ambiguities that define what they refer to as "states of security".

The last and fourth field that Samimian-Darash and Stalcup (2016) discuss is the one they propose and advocate for; namely the assemblage approach to security that includes "objects, concepts, and rationalities related to different security forms of action as well as the ethical mode of the anthropologist" (12). Abrahamsen and Williams (2009) already promoted such an approach earlier, and we understand that such a comprehensive approach seems both useful and attractive, as it specifically focuses on security actions and includes the various factors that define them, like we intend to do. However, because of its all-encompassing nature, the assemblage approach is, as we have argued elsewhere, too broad to act as a useful analytical tool to understand security practices in depth (Diphoorn and Grassiani 2016). Furthermore, an assemblage approach does not always adequately convey the ambiguities that emerge from policing. In contrast, the idea of security blurs aims to act as an analytical tool that emphasises the various opacities that are inherent to security practices.

Essentially, many of the contributions in this volume could use the security assemblage framework to analyse how various actors, objects, networks and rationalities come together to provide and/or create a sense of security (and Møhl explicitly uses this approach in her chapter). However, in this volume, we regard the assemblage as a prior assumption and go a step further by fleshing out the blurriness that defines so many security practices across the globe and that are observed within the assemblage approach, but not always investigated in detail. This means that we are not only interested in analysing the ways in which security assemblages emerge and exist, but that we are particularly attentive to the blurriness of its context, performance and effects as we will explain further below. In this way this book draws from all of the different bodies of work mentioned above, bringing forth dimensions of violence, militarism and non-state policing, and examines them in more depth through the security blurs that are intrinsically a part of them.

Security blurs

As hinted to in the previous section, we approach security as a performance; as an act that is identified, both by the actors doing it and those affected by it, as a form of "doing security". We want to stay away from defining security as an objective state of being that one can achieve (or does not manage to) and that carries a specific value in society. In fact, we share much of the critique (e.g. Neocleous and Rigakos 2011) against the habitual ways in which "security" has come to equate any form of (perceived) threat and thereby conjures sentiments of fear and uncertainty. We do not intend to reproduce such conventions of security. Yet despite this critique, many people across the globe identify themselves as security providers, as individuals who are involved in "doing" security and we cannot ignore this self-labelling. In the various case studies examined in this volume, individuals use security as a form of self-identification, for example, security actors who are making things, people and places safer. Security is thus very much an emic term that is used by our interlocutors, and conveys different meanings in various parts of the world. We therefore use the idea of security not to refer to an objective state that can be achieved, but as a subjective and self-identified label and act. And within these acts, towards some kind of subjective safe state of being for different actors, blurs emerge and occur – as both a process and as a state of being.

We define security blurs as manifestations of security that are visible and identifiable, yet in their inception and performance, they are constructed and made up of myriad overlapping sets of actors, roles, motivations, values, materialities and power dynamics. If we revisit the example from Tel Aviv, it is clear that security is being enacted; yet the different dynamics, relationships and constituents behind this enactment remain unclear at first sight. The security performance itself is therefore visible and recognisable, as something that has the aim of providing a sense of safety for a specific group of people, yet the processes and dynamics around the performance demand further investigation.

In order to further unravel such cases, we propose to employ a three-dimensional approach to analyse security blurs by focusing on three different, yet interrelated, simultaneous and fluid layers: the structural, the performative, and the effective. This entails that a blur emerges at its inception due to complex social structures and political dynamics (structural); continues through its performance by different actors, roles and objects (performative); and works through in the effect of its performance, namely on and through different audiences (effective). In each of the contributions to this volume, these three layers are present, yet some layers emerge more prominently in certain chapters than in others. In the following section, we will further discuss these layers by examining how they materialise throughout the chapters.

The structural layer

The structural layer refers to the larger context in which the security performance takes place. This includes the presence of various institutions (both formal and informal), legal frameworks, political and historical trajectories of power and domination, economic structures of power that define matters of class and financial opportunities and social conditions, such as race, ethnicity and gender, to name but a few, that determine the environment in which the security blur manifests itself. In the introductory example from Tel Aviv, for example, the structural layer of the performance refers to the existence of various institutions that are part of this patrolling initiative (the Tel Aviv municipality, the Israeli police and the private security company that provides guards for the patrols); the legal frameworks within which the patrol, the actors, and their duties and rights are embedded in and defined by, such as the laws determining firearm use and ownership and the extensive regulation system of the private security industry. Furthermore, it can include issues of inequalities surrounding the patrols in Israel in general, which only municipalities with certain financial capacities can afford.[3] We can even extend the analysis further by incorporating the larger geo-political context of Israel, and thereby include the occupation of Palestinian land and accompanying ideas about Palestinian (Arab) others and, for example, the thousands of African refugees who do not receive asylum and as such are exposed to inhumane conditions in Southern Tel Aviv. Combined, all of these dimensions and facets constitute the structural layer.

A chapter of this volume that highlights the structural layer is Jeremy Siegman's chapter on the blurring of civilian/military life. In his analysis of Super-Israel, a supermarket in an Israeli settlement in the occupied West Bank, he analyses the co-presence of violent military occupation and setter-colonialism that define Israel's militarised security and counter-terror apparatus, and he portrays how these political structures shape two blurred processes at the supermarket: the militarisation and civilianisation of security. Through his insightful ethnographic data, he portrays how private forms of security are used to not only normalise the Israeli occupation in everyday life, but also the settler presence that is part of it, even as the Israeli military apparatus comes into full view at times. Although Siegman's chapter is focused on everyday life, it nonetheless highlights the structural layer in a particular way: his operationalisation of terms such as "settler colonialism" and "military occupation" draw continued attention to how everyday life is shaped by these dominant structures, more bluntly than some of the other authors. Nonetheless, in their own ways, all the chapters demonstrate the importance of considering the wider context within which security performances take place.

The performative layer

With the performative layer, we are referring to the security act itself: to the performance of actual practices which includes the actors (state and non-state, armed and non-armed, formal and informal), their motivations and perceptions, and the various materialities that constitute the performance, such as cars, weapons, uniforms, documents and technologies. If we look again at the introductory example, we can identify the various actors involved in the performance; private guards employed by the municipality and police officers. We further recognise the role of the aesthetics of the vehicles, as the municipality patrol car closely resembles a regular police vehicle, and we can see how the uniforms of the different actors are almost similar. The role of the weapon is also important in this example; both actors can carry a weapon (in the case of the guards, this depends on their specific clearance by police and the ministry of defence), but they face different regulations concerning its use. The daily interactions between the dissimilar actors, the different sponsors they have (state and municipality), their use or disuse of specific objects, the way they use these objects and the negotiations surrounding their daily work can all be analysed as blurs.

Most of the contributions of this volume flesh out the security blurs at this performative layer, and portray how they occur across the various actors involved who habitually trespass across so-called borders of state versus non-state and informal versus formal. The chapter where blurs between security providers is most prevalent is that by Moritz Schuberth, who explicitly discusses the blurriness between various armed groups in Haiti. In addition to highlighting the problematic process by which these actors are labelled, which is often done by external actors, Schuberth shows the blurring between providers of security and providers of insecurity, who are often one and the same. He therefore proposes to shift our focus to the sponsors, rather than the producers of security, as this provides more insight into their motivations and makes it possible to discern security blurs.

In Perle Møhl's chapter on border security at Copenhagen airport, she describes the various actors and technologies operating at the airport as an unstable security assemblage and portrays the blurring of responsibilities, decision-making and ongoing negotiations between the human actors, and between human and non-human ones. She distinguishes between two types of blurs. The first occur on a structural level and this refers to the conflicting agendas and interests of the various actors, which appear coherent on the surface, but are in fact blurred and unclear. The second are blurs that occur in the particular instances where control authority is allocated and when decisions are made by the various actors. Combined, this chapter depicts how the presence of numerous actors and the overlapping and intermixing of roles, motivations, responsibilities and practices produce various forms of blurs.

Similarly, in Atreyee Sen's chapter, security blurs also merge through the co-production of (informal) policing activities, this time by resident women with strong Hindu nationalist sympathies, policemen and security guards in an effort to combat "loose girls" and the indecency they bring to the neighbourhoods. Sen shows how issues of responsibilisation become important within the community around questions about who is responsible of "security" and how is security defined (and by whom). In this case, the community members use the moral argument, as they believe that "immoral" behaviour of women will attract criminals, paedophiles and the like. In this chapter we do therefore not necessarily see a blurring among actors, but a blurring of their motivations and goals, making it unclear to identify who is steering policing practices and who will benefit from them in terms of (perceived) safety or status for example.

Sen's chapter also uncovers the crucial role of urban space in defining security blurs by comparing militant moral policing practices conducted in two different spaces – a bridge and a park. Through this analysis, she shows how violence and security are embodied and experienced in everyday urban space and how they impact spatio-temporal milieus that eventually develop gendered geographies of urban fear. The prominence of space is also crucial in areas that can be defined as frontier-like or as in-between settings, which often act as sites of power struggles between the state and non-state security actors working to keep certain groups out and civilians who either are rejected or embraced by the state. In Møhl's chapter, for example, the specific setting of the airport determines that the decision-making processes concerning access to the airport is tricky and unpredictable and that the threshold for facial recognition becomes blurry when machines take over the tasks of humans.

The role of machines is an example of the prominent role of security technologies in Møhl's chapter, where we cannot underestimate the decisive role that objects, materialities and technologies play in shaping the security blur, especially at the performative layer. We do not only learn more about crucial technologies, such as Automated Border Control (ABC) and algorithmic thresholds, but also about how individuals interact with such technologies (human and non-human) and how this interaction plays a crucial role in the blurring. Møhl, for example, shows how human agents at times disagree with the decisions of the machine and questions are raised about the qualities of risk assessments.

In addition to machines, other non-human entities that surface in several chapters are weapons: their use and at times the normalisation of their presence. The use of weapons, or the ability of individuals to carry arms, brings us to another important aspect within the performative layer of security acts: the centrality of violence, especially in conjuring and gaining legitimacy and authority. Although various forms of policing and security are non-violent, violence – or the potentiality of it – emerges in all of the chapters, either as physical violence or as more structural as "embedded in the political and economic organization of our social world" (Farmer et al. 2006: 1686).

This is particularly evident in Helene Maria Kyed's chapter on contested sovereignty in Maputo, Mozambique, where she analyses the entanglements between civilian and state policing and how this results in both the blurring of types of policing actors as well as a blurring of community-based and state police practices. By focusing on two empirical examples – the theft of a mobile phone and a police uniform ceremony – she shows how the policing roles of the civilian agents and state police officers constantly blur through mutual interdependencies, entanglements and exchanges, and how these practices are equally infused with ongoing competition over power, benefits and legitimacy. By use of these rich empirical examples, Kyed shows that violence is part of the routinised aspects of everyday policing and plays a crucial role in asserting positions of power and overcoming uncertainty. Here too, we observe the crucial role of materialities: in the police uniform ceremony, she describes how uniforms and batons were first given to civilian agents within the community-policing programme, but were then forbidden, as they would look too similar to "real" police officers. This not only shows the immense symbolic power of the uniform, but also highlights how issues of legitimacy and sovereignty foreground such a blur.

Finally, Line Jakobsen and Lars Buur's chapter also addresses matters of violence and insecurity, this time in urban peripheries in La Paz, Bolivia. In their contribution, they demonstrate how community-policing practices have become entangled with local informal vigilante-like practices of order-making, and how these entanglements are largely shaped by the use of violence. They address the implications of the translation of a global security technology into a local setting and examine how "order-making" takes place and security becomes blurred in this process of implementation. By drawing from numerous interviews with local residents, they show how fear and insecurity reigns in these urban peripheral communities. Therefore, while global community-policing "blueprints" were intended to reduce crime and provide "security", they have morphed into new policing practices and structures which tend to produce more insecurity. This facet reaffirms that security acts intrinsically have flip sides, and are always produced for *and* against someone, either an individual or collective, and this dimension is largely encapsulated in the third layer – the effective.

The effective layer

The effective layer refers to the effect of the security performance on the various actors involved. This includes the performers themselves (i.e. the security providers), but also the receivers, such as clients, members and citizens; both those that are "protected" and targeted. The main dimension of this effective layer concerns the feelings of safety, security, insecurity and feelings of uncertainty that can accompany security performances. To use the introductory example one last time, here one could investigate the way the public in the low-income neighbourhood perceives this patrol. Do some feel they are being targeted? Do others feel safer because of the visible patrols in the streets? And importantly, how does this work impact the security guards and the police officers accompanying them? Are certain ideas and skills transferred during such patrols? And does the cooperation change the status of the actors or the power relations between them? The answers to such questions are by definition fluid and should be analysed as processual and contextual. Only then, by examining such security blurs in detail, can we understand the security performance in its totality.

The chapter that addresses the effective layer head-on is the one by Laurens Bakker. In addition to examining the multitude of local security providers and the various roles that they claim and are ascribed, Bakker primarily analyses how such understandings of policing are infused with understandings of national citizenship and belonging. Furthermore, the *ormas* (societal organisations) play a pivotal role in deciding what and who is the "community", and thereby explicitly engage in exclusive practices, and how this results in a stratified form of citizenship. Bakker thus show how security providers are capable of setting conditions in terms of indigeneity, ethnicity, religion and locality, and how these elements impact upon the quality of citizenship of those affected.

In each of the contributions, we can clearly see that security acts prominently shape the lives of people in a multitude of ways. These can be the actual performers of security, such as the community policing agents in Maputo and La Paz, the security guards working at the Copenhagen airport, and the Hindu nationalist women in Mumbai; the citizens that live in neighbourhoods where policing practices are enacted, such as the residents of Maputo, the inhabitants of the *barrios* in La Paz, the people living in and working for non-governmental organisations in Port-au-Prince and of course, those that are specifically targeted by the security performance, such as the Palestinians working in Super-Israel, the "migrants" that are denied access to enter the Schengen area and the couples that are morally disciplined in various public spaces in Mumbai. Whether you are the performer, receiver, target or bystander of a security performance, it impacts you and this highlights the differentially effective dimension of the security blur.

Another key effect that emerges from most of the chapters and that is particularly well captured by ethnographic research is the production of uncertainty and "not knowing": due to the various forms of blurring, it is often not clear what exactly is happening and who is doing what. This dimension strongly emerges in Møhl's chapter, where it is often unclear who is responsible for the decisions that are made, especially for the users of the airport. Yet this also results in frustration by the providers and the border guards, and features in their interactions with the various objects. This dimension of not knowing who belongs to whom and not being able to identify the political alliances between the different actors is a big factor Schuberth's chapter. This uncertainty is a crucial component of the effective domain of security blurs, and reaffirms the need to unpack them.

A note on ethnography

A final note we wish to make concerns the ethnographic dimension of this volume, which we believe ties all of the chapters together. All of the authors that contributed to this volume conducted in-depth ethnographic fieldwork in their respective localities. This is clearly evident from the rich empirical data that is presented – not only do we see abundant quotes from interviews, but also conversations and discussions between individuals, and extensive notes deriving from participant observation. The thick descriptions that are offered by the authors not only provide in-depth analytical perspectives, but also demonstrate the benefits from longitudinal research visits that are often conducted by anthropologists.

It is not our intention here to equate ethnographic fieldwork with anthropology, or to assume that ethnographic fieldwork is similarly understood and exercised by all of the contributors to this volume. In fact, the diverse forms of data portrayed here point towards the various ways in which we employ certain methods, the type of data that is yielded from such methods, and the way we use, interpret and analyse this data. Furthermore, we also do not wish to claim that an anthropological approach to security solely rests of ethnographic fieldwork.

However, we do want to emphasise that ethnographic fieldwork, in its various forms and styles, acts as a crucial tool in identifying, observing and analysing security blurs. Ethnographic fieldwork is a key dimension to understanding the core of any security performance and fully unravelling how the various layers – structural, performative and effective – take shape and emerge (see Hansen 2018). Some of the key facets that define ethnographic fieldwork are longitudinal stays and re-visits, learning the local language/dialect, understanding tacit elements of people's behaviour, observing and participating with people in their everyday affairs, taking extensive notes of these observations, experiences and emotions, engaging in small talk, and conducting diverse types of interviews with people. These are all methods and techniques that allow the researcher to actually be present at the security performances and see the blurs come into being with her own eyes. It is primarily for this reason that we hope this volume will assist us in further developing an anthropological approach to security that is also beneficial for scholars outside the discipline.

Notes

1 This is a description by the first author.
2 www.tel-aviv.gov.il/About/Pages/SELA.aspx, accessed May 25 2018.
3 www.calcalist.co.il/local/articles/0,7340,L-3645934,00.html, accessed May 30 2018.

References

Abrahamsen, Rita, and Michael C. Williams. 2009. "Security Beyond the State: Global Security Assemblages in International Politics". *International Political Sociology* 3 (1): 1–17.

Albrecht, Peter. 2016. "Hybridisation in a Case of Diamond Theft in Rural Sierra Leone". *Ethnos.* https://doi.org/10.1080/00141844.2016.1263229.

Albrecht, Peter, and Helene Maria Kyed, eds. 2015. *Policing and the Politics of Order-Making.* New York: Routledge.

Bakker, Laurens. 2015. "Illegality for the General Good? Vigilantism and Social Responsibility in Contemporary Indonesia". *Critique of Anthropology* 35 (1): 78–93.

Ben-Ari, Eyal. 1998. *Mastering Soldiers: Conflict, Emotions and the Enemy in an Israeli Military Unit.* New York: Berghahn Books.

Buur, Lars. 2006. "Reordering Society: Vigilantism and Expressions of Sovereignty in Port Elizabeth's Townships". *Development and Change* 37 (4): 735–757.

Caldeira, Teresa P.R. 2000. *City of Walls: Crime, Segregation, and Citizenship in Sao Paulo.* Berkeley: University of California Press.

Colona, Francesco, and Rivke Jaffe. 2016. "Hybrid Governance Arrangements". *The European Journal of Developmental Research* 28 (2): 175–183.

Denyer Willis, Graham. 2015. *The Killing Consensus: Police, Organised Crime and the Regulation of Life and Death in Urban Brazil.* Berkeley: University of California Press.

Diphoorn, Tessa. 2016. *Twilight Policing: Private Security and Violence in Urban South Africa.* Berkeley: University of California Press.

Diphoorn, Tessa, and Erella Grassiani. 2016. "Securitizing Capital: A Processual-Relation Approach to Pluralised Security". *Theoretical Criminology* 20 (4): 430–445.

Diphoorn, Tessa, and Helene Maria Kyed. 2016. "Entanglements of Private Security and Community Policing in South Africa and Swaziland". *African Affairs* 115 (461): 710–732.

Farmer, Paul, Bruce Nizeye, Sara Stulac, and Salmaan Keshavjee. 2006. "Structural Violence and Clinical Medicine". *PLoS Med* 3 (10): e449.

Fassin, Didier. 2013. *Enforcing Order: An Ethnography of Urban Policing.* Cambridge: Polity Press.

Fassin, Didier, ed. 2017. *Writing the World of Policing: The Difference Ethnography Makes*. Chicago: University of Chicago Press.

Feldman, Alan. 1991. *Formations of Violence: The Narrative of the Body and Political Terror in Northern Ireland*. Chicago: Chicago University Press.

Garriot, William, ed. 2013. *Policing and Contemporary Governance: The Anthropology of Police in Practice*. New York: Palgrave MacMillan.

Glück, Zoltán, and Setha Low. 2017. "A Sociospatial Framework for the Anthropology of Security". *Anthropological Theory* 17 (3): 281–296.

Goldstein, Daniel. 2010. "Toward a Critical Anthropology of Security". *Current Anthropology* 51 (4): 487–517.

Grassiani, Erella. 2013. *Soldering Under Occupation: Processes of Numbing Among Israel Soldiers in the Al-Aqsa Intifada*. New York: Berghahn Books.

Grassiani, Erella, and Lior Volinz. 2016. "Intimidation, Reassurance, and Invisibility: Israeli Security Agents in the Old City of Jerusalem". *Focaal* 75: 14–30.

Hansen, Rebecca. 2018. "Ethnographies of Security: Pushing Security Studies Beyond the Bounds of International Relations". *Qualitative Sociology*: 1–7. https://doi.org/10.1007/s11133-018-9384-0.

Higate, Paul, and Mats Utas, eds. 2017. *Private Security in Africa: From the Global Assemblage to the Everyday*. London: Zed Books.

Hurtado, Fina Anton, and Giovanni Ercolani. 2013. *Anthropology and Security Studies*. Univesidad de Murcia, Nottingham Trent University and College of William and Mary.

Jauregui, Beatrice. 2016. *Provisional Authority: Police, Order, and Security in India*. Chicago: University of Chicago Press.

Jensen, Steffen. 2008. *Gangs, Politics and Dignity in Cape Town*. Oxford: James Currey.

Karpiak, Kevin. 2010. "Of Heroes and Polemics: 'The Policemen in Urban Ethnography'". *Political and Legal Anthropology Review* 33 (1): 7–31.

Kyed, Helene Maria. 2009. "Community Policing in Post-war Mozambique. *Policing and Society* 19 (4): 354–371.

Larkins, Erika Robb. 2017. "Guarding the Body: Private Security Work in Rio de Janeiro". *Conflict and Society* 3 (1): 61–72.

Low, Setha. 2013. "Securitization Strategies: Gated Communities and Market-rate Co-operatives in New York". In *Policing Cities: Urban Securitization and Regulation in a 21st Century World*, edited by Randy K. Lippert and Kevin Walby, 222–230. London: Routledge.

Maguire, Mark, Catarina Frois, and Nils Zurawski, eds. 2014. *The Anthropology of Security: Perspectives from the Frontline of Policing, Counter-terrorism and Border Control*. London: Pluto Press.

Mynster Christensen, Maya. 2017. "Shadow Soldiering: Shifting Constellations and Permeable Boundaries in 'Private' Security Contracting". *Conflict and Society* 3 (1): 24–41.

Neocleous, Mark, and George S. Rigakos, eds. 2011. *Anti-Security*. Ottawa: Red Quill Books.

Nordstrom, Carolyn, and Antonius C.G.M. Robben, eds. 1995. *Fieldwork Under Fire: Contemporary Studies of Violence and Survival*. Berkeley: University of California Press.

Pedersen, Axel Morten, and Martin Holbraad, eds. 2013. *Times of Security: Ethnographies of Fear, Protest and the Future*. London: Routledge.

Pratten, David, and Atryee Sen, eds. 2007. *Global Vigilantes*. London: Hurst & Company.

Rodgers, Dennis. 2006. "The State as a Gang: Conceptualizing the Governmentality of Violence in Contemporary Nicaragua". *Critique of Anthropology* 26 (3): 315–330.

Ruteere, Mutuma, and Marie-Emmanuelle Pommerolle. 2003. "Democratizing Security or Decentralizing Repression? The Ambiguities of Community Policing in Kenya". *African Affairs* 102: 587–604.

Samimian-Darash, Limor, and Meg Stalcup. 2016. "Anthropology of Security and Security in Anthropology: Cases of Terrorism in the United States". *Anthropological Theory* 17 (1): 60–87.

Scheper-Hughes, Nancy, and Philippe Bourgois, eds. 2004. *Violence in War and Peace: An Anthology*. Oxford: Blackwell Publishing.

Van Stapele, Naomi. 2015. *Respectable 'Illegality': Gangs, Masculinities, and Belonging in a Nairobi Ghetto*. PhD Dissertation, University of Amsterdam.

Winslow, Donna. 1997. *The Canadian Airborne Regiment in Somalia: A Socio-Cultural Inquiry: A Study Prepared for the Commission of Inquiry Into the Deployment of Canadian Forces to Somalia*. Ottawa: The Commission.

1 "The supermarket became an army base!"

Security and the military/civilian blur in an Israeli settlement

Jeremy Siegman

Introduction

This chapter explores Israel's settler-colonial project, and its relevance for broader questions about liberalism, war and security, through a focus rather distinct from the typical icons of military rule such as the Separation Barrier and checkpoints: the discount supermarket chains that have proliferated in Israeli settlements in recent years. Here shelf-stocking, cleaning and other entry-level service jobs are mostly done by Palestinians from nearby towns under variations of military occupation. The stores are under heavy – but complex – forms of security. One of the key initial observations of my ethnographic work, which focused on one settlement supermarket which I call Super-Israel, in a large settlement just outside Jerusalem, was how distinct some aspects of security there were from the broader militarised landscape in which this and similar stores were located.[1] At the store entrance, private guards wore polo shirts rather than the fatigues seen at military checkpoints a few kilometres away; they greeted customers and other workers in a friendly way, including, occasionally, Palestinians, in contrast to the simple and often gruff commands of soldiers at checkpoints. Pistols subtly hung on their belts rather than the M-16s of soldiers. They checked bags on the way in, usually in cursory fashion, and receipts on the way out. As I would soon learn, on one level, security provision at the store ostensibly prioritised preventing theft. And security at the store, at first blush, seemed to align with a mundane and cheery atmosphere oriented towards consumer satisfaction. Thus, in the context of my broader inquiry into the political significance of Israeli-Palestinian encounter at these supermarkets, I became interested in the reconfiguration of Israeli security from a military paradigm to an ostensibly private, civilian one as one way in which these market encounters serve to normalise settler presence and military occupation in everyday life. Yet the picture is a bit more complicated. Indeed, the installation of ostensibly private, non-militarised forms of security within a landscape of military occupation is an inherently partial process that generates a blurring between the military and the civilian, among other ambiguities.

Thus I argue in this chapter that there is a tension and an ongoing vacillation between two tendencies of Israeli security at Super-Israel, and more broadly in the service economy of Israel's Jerusalem-area frontiers. On the one hand, there is a partial civilianisation of security – evident, for example, in the attire and behaviour of the private guards I have mentioned – that furthers the normalisation of Israeli settler life as dominant in the West Bank. It does so not by erasing military occupation but rather by creating a consumer-focused atmosphere in which occupation, and political dynamics relating to it, are pushed to the background of everyday experience, especially for Jewish-Israeli customers. On the other hand, there is a re-militarisation of security, in which the continuity and inseparability of the military and the civilian are performed and acknowledged with varying degrees of openness, allowing political tensions to come to the fore and unsettle the aforementioned normalisation of settler life. For example, even if the security guards at the stores are not acting as soldiers, they have been soldiers or continue to serve as reserve soldiers; moreover, many customers *are* on-duty or off-duty soldiers or members of other security agencies, stopping to get food for their bases or nearby homes; they carry pistols and M-16 assault rifles as they shop, producing occasional stares or coldness from Palestinian workers. And of course, there are military jeeps in the parking lot, and checkpoints and jeeps on the adjacent roads. Moreover, the whole arrangement of employing Palestinians who live under military rule relies on intense forms of monitoring that ostensibly occur out of view of customers and most workers, in which store managers cooperate with the Israeli military agency which issues workers' permits, and the *shabak* (the Hebrew acronym for the Israeli internal security services, also commonly known in English by the Hebrew initials Shin Bet).[2]

These ostensibly hidden forms of militarised policing structure everyday interactions in the store through suspicion, and are implicitly acknowledged in the store in various ways.[3] And at times, civilian managers and even customers brazenly perform themselves and others (including the ethnographer) as potential or actual extensions of Israel's militarised security apparatus. Here, the Israeli counter-terror apparatus operates with a boundless effect, always haunting the prospect of civilian personhood, space and time: any Israeli can function as security personnel, whether formally deputised by the state (as some are in the settlements) or not; any Palestinian, and Palestinian-ness itself, can become a target; and this can happen at any time, so long as Palestinians are present either physically or as a present absence, an imagined threat. In emergency situations, managers may help detain Palestinians, including workers, in cooperation with the state security apparatus, and the anticipation and aftermath of these moments of emergency shapes everyday practice in expansive ways, far beyond isolated incidents themselves.

Taken together, and drawing on Masco's (2014) account of U.S. national security affect, we might theorise the tensions between these tendencies of security at Super-Israel as an open circuit, from modes of normalcy in which latent suspicion simmers, sometimes brazenly acknowledged, to modes of escalation, antagonism and violence, and then back to a fragile normalcy that remains vulnerable to unravelling.[4] The blurring of different forms of security is essential to this whole circuit – to the possibility of normalisation at Super-Israel, its fragility, and its intermittent undoing. For example, as noted, this normalisation is partial in the first place, adorned with military accoutrements, suspicions and brazen performances of its fragility. My argument thus draws on Anthropology and Critical International Relations literatures on a global blurring between military and civilian forms of power (Duffield 2001; Lutz 2002; Jauregui 2010; Bachmann et al. 2014), for example the militarisation of ostensibly civilian policing. Israel and other settler-colonial projects entail profound forms of security blurring, as ongoing forms of colonial and military violence and related forms of racialisation (Camp and Heatherton 2016) shape social and political life on both external frontiers and the "homefront" (Lutz 2002; Rana 2014; Masco 2014), including in mundane, ostensibly civilian contexts such as a supermarket. An account of this blurring can move us beyond a narrow focus on Israeli military occupation itself, advancing a recent push by scholars to situating the occupation within broader dynamics of Israeli settler colonisation (Salamanca et al. 2012) and contributing a distinctive ethnographic focus on everyday Israeli-Palestinian forms of contact to this settler colonialism scholarship.

My account also converses with recent anthropologies of security, especially a recent literature that, influenced by Science Studies, has focused on security as an object of knowledge and intervention by proliferating apparatuses of governance, population management, and expert knowledge (Lakoff 2008; Masco 2014; O'Neill 2015; cf. Khalili 2012). This framework, in Foucauldian fashion, shows how such apparatuses undermine agentive politics and democratic contestation (Hall 2012), focusing on logics of governance, for example as found in U.S. and other counter-insurgency manuals (Kelly et al. 2010; Khalili 2012). I am interested in another direction in Masco's work (2014), which explores not only the constitution of security apparatuses and the politics they suppress, but in the forms of collective affect, belonging and friend/enemy relations (cf. Schmitt 2007) that they mobilise. Building as well on other anthropologies of security that highlight instability and complex interactions between various actors (cf. Goldstein 2012; Feldman 2015) in the field of everyday practice, my ethnography draws attention to the ambiguous ideological effects of a dominant security project, including the ways that it can at times further dynamics of everyday instability and undermine the normalisation of a dominant order.

My account is based on 18 months of ethnographic research, centred on 6 months of intensive participant observation at Super-Israel as a cashier, deli worker and stocker.[5] The complexities of negotiating access to a space where I clearly was not a typical participant, but had affiliations with the dominant group, helped attune me to the forms of suspicion that simmered there, especially during the escalations before and after the 2014 Gaza assault – insights that would become central to my argument. At the same time, I was able to gain detailed insights into how both settlers and Palestinians acted in, and reflected on, their everyday commercial contact, including by developing trust and eventually friendship with a number of Palestinian workers. After I stopped working at Super-Israel, I complemented my observations there with continued immersion in the Palestinian workers' lives. I also worked with a Jerusalemite Palestinian researcher and activist, to conduct further interviews with West Bank and Jerusalemite Palestinians who had worked service and other jobs in the settlements and Jerusalem.

The chapter proceeds, roughly, from showing how military occupation is partially civilianised at Super-Israel, to the various ways that the attendant military/civilian blurring generates forms of suspicion and tension in everyday life at the supermarket, culminating in a discussion of how these everyday forms of tension relate to more eruptive moments of militarisation and violence.

Civilianising military occupation

On their way to work, whether in their own cars or in the company van, Palestinians encounter various military checkpoints, which focus specifically on regulating their movement and not settlers'. But at the gate to the settlement industrial zone where this Super-Israel branch is located, as with the gates to this and many other settlements, we begin to shift from a zone of military security to one of ostensibly private security. There is a private security checkpoint here, where yellow-plated Israeli cars are waved through by guards wearing T-shirts and flak jackets and carrying either pistols or assault rifles.[6] As at military checkpoints on settler routes, the guards appear to pay little attention to cars whose plates and passengers look Jewish-Israeli, for whom a quick nod or "shalom" in Hebrew is enough to get through. When I tried to give rides through the checkpoint to Palestinian workers, I was occasionally able to get them through without having to show their papers, but was sometimes stopped and chided in Hebrew, while the guards asked the workers for their permits or made them get out and go to their separate pedestrian-only lane – one of those micro-forms of segregation one finds throughout the West Bank (cf. Weizman 2007). This lane is essentially a sidewalk next to the road, with a small booth for a guard to stand in. There is no covering for the workers from the desert sun while they wait for a guard to come to the booth (the checkpoint often seems understaffed) – only a blue-painted railing that subtly separates those standing there from the road, and seems to double as a decorative touch, along with the reasonably well-maintained plantings in the road's median.

These checkpoints are sites of micro-political negotiation and antagonism among a settler and indigenous population who see each other every day – negotiations that continue between the workers and various Israelis inside the store. The guards are stern and sometimes cruel, other times matter of fact, but rarely as polite or friendly as some of the store managers can be. Getting slowed down at these checkpoints angers Ziad, a Jerusalemite Palestinian who works at the butcher counter and rides back to Jerusalem with me some days. "Them? Dogs!" he says, as we approach the industrial zone checkpoint and they check the IDs of the people in the car in front of us. He lives in Eissawiya, a neighbourhood just down the hill from Hebrew University that is surrounded on-and-off by checkpoints and blockades throughout my fieldwork, as clashes erupt between local youth and Israeli forces. The barriers make it difficult for me to drop off and pick up Ziad.

At the Super-Israel store entrance, security begins to feel different from out on the highways and even from the private checkpoint at the industrial zone entrance. There is not a full checkpoint here, just a private security guard wearing a polo shirt and khakis, sitting on a chair by the automatic doors with a pistol in his belt, like at a supermarket "anywhere in Israel", as settlers from this settlement would say. His profile is distinctly more casual than the guards at the industrial zone entrance. He casually glances at or barely opens people's bags as they come in, including Jewish-Israelis', and makes small talk with both Jewish-Israelis and Palestinians, as workers linger nearby while clocking in or out. The guard is often a middle-aged Jewish-Israeli from the former Soviet Union, with a firm handshake and a yarmulke, who chats informally with me.

The *kabatim*, or branch security officers, both have experience in the Israeli military. One *kabat*, Noam, is doing reserve duty when I arrive in the summer of 2014, as part of mass deployments for the ongoing Gaza assault (he is filling in elsewhere for soldiers deployed to Gaza). The other, Yotam, is applying for a job in the Israel Police.

But their role at Super-Israel is ostensibly private. They sometimes wear the white, long-sleeve button down shirts that other managers do, while other times they wear plain clothes.

A key emphasis in the *kabatim*'s security orientations for cashiers is how to prevent theft by workers or customers. This seems to be the ostensible focus and most common use of the many cameras throughout the store, although when it comes to the violent incidents mentioned below, the footage is taken and used by state security forces. In my new employee orientation, Yotam shows me how he can tell if someone tries to sneak merchandise around the cashiers, saying that if workers are caught stealing, "that's it, you go home". This disciplinary approach shapes the store's relation to both working-class Jewish-Israelis and to Palestinians, as would pertain in contemporary capitalist workplaces in many contexts. But not only are Palestinians disproportionately targeted by these forms of discipline, and disproportionately present in the lowest-level jobs where they would be targeted (while the managers are almost all Jewish-Israeli); they are the sole targets of many more layers of security here, in which the civilian and the military realms, as well as those of class and ethno-nationality, are profoundly blurred.

State security forces' involvement with Israeli businesses and Palestinian labour

My interviews with workers at this store and in a range of Israeli service jobs add texture to other accounts of how the Israeli army's Civil Administration, the Israel Police and the *shabak* are heavily involved in policing Palestinians, including Palestinian workers, in the Jerusalem region on both sides of the Green Line; one key intervention here is to show how these forms of policing connect the state to various civilian Israeli actors – not only employers but private security officers and even customers.[7] On one level, even as this involvement with the workers is both potent and expansive, incorporating various Israeli actors, it often stays in the background of everyday practice at the supermarket and similar workplaces; this is fitting, for much of it is conducted by a quasi-secret agency, the *shabak*.

The army's Civil Administration, with involvement from the *shabak* (as well as administrative cooperation from the Palestinian Authority), administers work permits to a number of Palestinians from the West Bank, which they need in order to work in settlements or inside Israel. These permits provide powerful leverage against Palestinians for these state agencies and their employers alike, helping to suppress labour organising, exploit a vulnerable workforce (Bornstein 2002) and sometimes to entrap and recruit vulnerable workers to become collaborators with the *shabak*. *Shabak* agents may threaten to withdraw the necessary "security clearance" for workers' permits if they refuse to inform on their neighbours or family members, or simply because of other minor infractions against the occupation's rules, such as building without permits in Palestinian communities that are under full Israeli control (cf. Kelly 2009; Berda 2017). And because of the broader economic suffocation and insecurity Palestinians experience in the West Bank, losing a work permit for the Israeli economy can mean having to work for a third to half the wage for a similar job in the West Bank Palestinian economy. For Jerusalemite Palestinians, who are permanent residents of Israel but live under a *de facto* police state, the authorities and companies similarly exploit their vulnerability, which is also deepened by economic suffocation, albeit to a somewhat lesser degree for some.

This system works well enough to suppress labour violation complaints to Israeli courts and organisations that I never heard the Super-Israel workers from the West Bank mention this option, despite rampant violations of Israeli labour law in settlement businesses' employment of Palestinians (Kadman 2012). When I finally brought up these mechanisms for redress after a number of months, workers said things like, "are you kidding? You complain and boom, no permit!" The situation was similar with regard to labour organising, which I never heard West Bank workers mention. Jerusalemites spoke of some proud walkouts but rarely mentioned being members of unions or full-fledged organising efforts.

State policing interventions vis-à-vis workers could often begin with theft as a pre-text, quickly escalating into entrapment as part of a broader, racially inflected project of policing backed by the power of a military occupation. For example, one worker told me a story of a West Bank Palestinian who was stopped by police on his way home from work and accused of having stolen a small item. The *shabak* said that if he did not collaborate with them he would lose his permit. He came to other workers and they advised him not to cooperate. Other stories involved direct communication between Israeli authorities and private *kabatim* at the stores, in which the latter fired workers without cause after they had merely been questioned by police or *shabak*.

Workers had stories like this of interrogations going back decades, to when most of them worked inside Jerusalem and Israel. In the 1990s, with Israel's policy of closure, permits became harder to get and enforcement got stricter; Palestinians' illicit daily commutes became more dangerous, their employment even more precarious, and eventually many could no longer work inside the Israeli areas, experiencing economic freefall as a result. Other workers I knew were temporarily or permanently fired after the Israeli authorities withdrew their work permits, for reasons such as a family member refusing to become a collaborator.

Palestinians were aware of ongoing communications between the *kabatim* and state authorities, as well as the fact that many *kabatim* were past or future police officers or soldiers. This awareness bred suspicion. One Palestinian worker with decades of experience said, "there is direct communication between the security officers and the *shabak*", adding "the *kabat* at a store isn't just a guy off the street. He has reached a certain level in the *shabak*. He was probably working there and then had to stop for some reason, maybe he retired, maybe he was injured". Though I did not further pursue this specific claim, the *kabatim* I encountered did at a minimum have ongoing ties to other branches of the security forces, and conducted their own forms of surveillance upon the workers that mimicked state practices.

Again, these forms of pressure and intimidation generally remained out of view of daily life at the store, particularly out of view of most customers. Indeed, the stories I have shared here mostly come from interviews conducted outside the store.

Public secrecy, brazenness and suspicion

Yet these forms of security entailed forms of performance, everyday interaction and dynamics of suspicion that did come up in the store and affect its social atmosphere. For example, Palestinian workers sometimes expressed, in the store, awareness of the ways they were being monitored, and suspicion about not only *kabatim*, but Israeli managers, co-workers and even customers taking part. Indeed, when remarking upon how they were monitored – or might be monitored – Palestinian workers often took for granted the interchangeability of supermarket managers, branch security officers, some customers and state security. The workers considered various Jewish-Israeli colleagues and some Palestinians as well to be potential or actual "spies" [Ar. *jawasees*]. Sometimes they specified that they meant spies for the boss, other times for the state, and other times it was left unclear.

The prospect of Jewish-Israeli managers or customers speaking Arabic was a major factor in making Palestinians suspicious of them. A Palestinian citizen of Israel with decades of experience working for Israelis said in a suspicious tone that many company security officers "know Arabic very well, Mizrahi and Ashkenazi. One came to me and joked about *sifara fil imara* with Adel Imam!" We laughed at the notion that the officers knew Arabic so well that they watched popular Egyptian movies. Given the context of the conversation, the man was pointing to these Israelis' knowledge of Arabic as something threatening to Palestinians even as it was banal.

Workers even suspected customers, often expressing this suspicion as part of their banal frustration with them. When Palestinian workers spoke to each other in Arabic or played Palestinian music at the deli counter or registers, Jewish-Israeli customers usually looked on blankly. Palestinians were unsure if these "unratified listeners" (Goffman 1981) were merely customers anxious to be served or malicious eavesdroppers. Yusuf, a genial deli-slicer who often slapped hands with macho Jewish-Israeli customers, surprised me with how matter-of-factly dark his interpretation was: "they all understand Arabic, I'm telling you – they just pretend they don't to see if you're talking about them".

As an example of what Israeli customers' monitoring of Palestinian workers could mean, a worker named Muhammad told me angrily about how one customer complained that a Palestinian worker's Islamic-style beard made him look "suspicious"; the customer evidently had called the police or the *shabak* and the worker lost his permit soon after.

The suspicion was mutual, even if its effects were by no means symmetrical. Jewish-Israelis openly expressed to me their own suspicion of (or sometimes just their ill regard for) Palestinians, both in interviews outside the store, and even at the store, within earshot of Palestinians, with a brazenness that surprised me. One of the handful of Jewish-Israeli female stockers who seemed unsettled by my closeness to the Palestinian workers started lecturing me right near some of them: "we can't trust the Palestinians, they aren't partners for peace. Here, they're good because they're dependent on the job. But in secret [Heb. *b'chadrei chadarim*], who knows what they're saying. . . ".

For the Palestinians' part, the assumption was that Israeli policing of Palestinians here was so pervasive, so totalising, so powerful that there was no point in trying to hide from it, just as Israelis themselves often made little effort to hide it, as we will see in a moment. For example, during a visit to an apartment rented during the week by quasi-migrant workers from Hebron, a worker asked to friend me on Facebook. I said I was not adding any of the workers in order to protect their anonymity. He was neither the first nor the last to laugh at or fail to understand this security practice of mine. "But they know everything about us!" he said. "They know when you come and when you go, they know who your friends are . . . so what's the point of trying to hide anything?" Indeed, the idea that I could help maintain any kind of security for the workers by maintaining their anonymity became more and more flimsy as I went on.

This Palestinian logic of giving up on trying to hide anything was not only a response to the overwhelming power of Israeli surveillance, but also part of a shared set of dynamics between Israelis and Palestinians regarding this surveillance: a variety of the public secret (Taussig 1999; Masco 2014). What public secrecy meant here was that things that were ostensibly secret, or conducted out of view of the public – state and corporate actors' monitoring of Palestinian workers – were sometimes openly and brazenly performed, especially for the Palestinian targets of this monitoring.

One form of such brazen performances was the way that Israeli workers and customers openly gestured at recruiting *me* into potential security roles, right in front of Palestinians.[8] These various kinds of informal recruitment pitches were based on the ways in which my positioning left me open to being interpellated as a Jewish-Israeli or someone aligned with Jewish-Israelis (cf. Verdery 2014).

For example, one day during the Gaza war, I was stocking yogurts with Hamdan, a Palestinian, when Tal, a skinny, brash Jewish-Israeli sales rep, arrived to deliver his shipment. In between going over inventories with Hamdan, Tal began taunting him about the ongoing Gaza war, identifying Hamdan with Hamas in a playful but provocative way. Tal then heard me speaking Arabic to Hamdan, and tried to pull me into this dynamic of antagonism, in which any Jewish-Israeli could be understood not only as supportive of, but as a potential *part* of the state security apparatus. "Oh, you speak Arabic?" he said. "Yeah", I said flatly, sensing some unwanted interpellation on the way. "Oh!" he said.

And with Hamdan right next to us, he launched into a recruitment speech of why I should work for the *shabak*: ". . . it's easy, it's a good salary, they just call you up and say 'hey, we need to go nab someone in Ramallah', and you go in there early in the morning, and you're home for lunch" – talking about a violent arrest raid like a casual outing, and doing so boldly in front of someone who lived in a town where such raids were common. Before he left, he took me aside and said, "really, think about it, it's a good deal". I tried the approach I saw Hamdan take: stoically nodding, faintly smiling and not really responding to the substance of the overture.

This episode was a playful, brazenly open performance of the *shabak*'s "secret" work, in front of someone from the population it targets. It made clear the publicly secret status of the *shabak* here – that part of its power comes from the productive tension between its work being clandestine on the one hand, and everyone knowing that it is happening, and that it can target Palestinians at any time, on the other. The status of the *shabak* here mirrored the status of occupation and conflict more broadly: plainly visible but filtered out at times; or on the other hand, ostensibly secret but bluntly spoken of, perhaps with a kind of over-the-top or even humorous twist that somehow made certain things more sayable.

The ways I was performed as part of a blurring between Israeli civilians and security forces here suggested how little space this blurring left for cross-national relationships. Indeed, for Tal and the customer alike, it did not matter if my speaking Arabic to Palestinians indexed any kind of relationship of solidarity; from a perspective such as Tal's, exchanges of kind words with a Palestinian would not be in contradiction with the taken-for-granted assumption that any Jewish-Israeli man would be being willing to serve in security forces that target (he would have said protect against) Palestinian populations. Within such an imaginary, a kind of cross-national solidarity that trumps fealty to Jewish-Israeli nationalism would most likely be understood largely as a form of treason.

The national element of these security performances also intersected with classed and gendered aspects bound up in my positioning in an Ashkenazi, university-educated, not very macho sort of masculinity. Indeed, Tal proposed a particular kind of security job that might be identified with the working-class, Mizrahi world he seemed to come from and that predominated at this Super-Israel: that of the *mist'arvim*, or Israeli units that pose as Palestinians in order to infiltrate Palestinian spaces and conduct raids – units which have often been manned by *mizrahi* Israeli populations. This was also an attempt to interpellate me into a particular kind of Jewish-Israeli masculinity: that of being an armed soldier who nonchalantly carries out military raids before lunch.

A more straightforward form of brazenly performing the military civilian/blur was the way Shlomo, the head manager, surveilled the workers. His office was on an elevated platform overlooking the store, next to the security office. His office had one-way glass windows, and one of its most notable features was a 50-something inch state-of-the-art plasma TV screen on the wall, which was most often used to review security tape.

This kind of surveillance was panoptical in a sense. But it also brought out the performative dimensions of panoptical security, complicating a foundational principle of the panopticon and of clandestine security – that the officer sees but is not seen. For workers could see the screen from the deli when the office windows were open, while Shlomo called in the security officer to zoom in on blurry stills from around the store. One day Yaser gestured up to the open window where the managers were reviewing some tape. In his characteristically non-confrontational and playful voice, he simply said, "they're watching tape" – registering that he was seeing that he was being seen, and registering that this was unfortunate, and perhaps also that there was nothing he could do about it.

In fact, Shlomo had a habit of disregarding the one-way glass and simply standing in the open window, looking down at the workers. Workers were keenly attuned to his presence and the presence of his deputies [Heb. *sganim*] who roved the store. The brazenness of these performances of surveillance in the workplace, and Palestinians' keen awareness and suspicion regarding this surveillance, once again suggests a paradoxical form of public secrecy. Michael Taussig (1999) and other scholars emphasise how the public secret serves to perform the power of the state in ways that magnify its mystery and allure – an insight that would be helpful in making sense of the vast power that Israeli security forces exercise over Palestinians in such settings. Yet my interest here is equally in how Israelis' performances of Israeli domination in such brazen, excessive ways might also unsettle a crucial aspect of Israeli power in the West Bank today: namely, the degree to which that power can be taken for granted in everyday life. For these brazen Israeli performances of the military/civilian blur stoked not only the Palestinian suspicions we have already seen, but occasionally mocking dramatisations of this blur, which I will detail in a moment.

Palestinian dramatisations of the Israeli military/civilian blur

Palestinians further dramatised the military/civilian blur, and its publicly secret qualities, through parodic performances, as part of a broader performative politics of antagonism in the supermarket.

For example, one day I was slicing deli meat when I heard from above me: "Jerman!"[9] I looked up and there was Muhammad, chest puffed out, standing in Shlomo the manager's one-way glass window as Shlomo often did. He gave me a little military salute as he often did, and the whole deli department was giggling and energised. Here was Muhammad, whom the workers called the *sheikh*, mimicking the store manager and a generic soldier figure all at once. Like Fanon's colonised subject but in a playful mode, he was portraying himself "in the place of the colonist" (2004), and with great results from his audience.

Yusuf yelled up to the window: "what's up, ya *m'alim*?" the latter term connoting both the word's meanings of "boss" or more generally "man" – hence the *sheikh* from Hebron playing boss of Super-Israel. "Send us our salaries!" Yusuf yelled up. "I'll send you police!" Muhammad yelled back. Now Muhammad blended the figure of Israeli police into his already composite character of manager-soldier.

Here, Muhammad and Yusuf openly and playfully drew out the brazenness of Shlomo's monitoring into an enactment of this monitoring as bound up in a military occupation. On one level, they acknowledged the unacknowledged aspect of this public secret, unmasking it at least for each other, and with the risky possibility that managers or customers could hear them, which would likely lead to disciplinary action from the store. This possibility itself gave such a performance its exhilarating, antagonistic quality. At the same time, the playfulness of their performance indexed the fact that making a serious, direct complaint was hardly thinkable. They thus enacted the simultaneous power and instability of this security arrangement, pushing its already unstable buttons without fundamentally undoing it.

Of course, there were less spectacular ways in which Palestinians registered the excessiveness of these Israeli security arrangements. When Palestinian workers were on break together or socialising on the job and managers would come, the workers would give each other little signals to pre-empt being yelled at or punished by at least appearing busy; for the managers they had Arabic code words which could be uttered matter-of-factly, with chuckles, or with just the slightest knowing glance or smile. This was a kind of small-scale security from below (cf. Goldstein 2012), where Palestinians cooperated with one another to protect livelihoods and social and national integrity as colonised people under threat. Despite the Palestinian workers' social ties being constantly compromised by the management's installation of hierarchy between them (e.g. picking favourites, giving preferential bonuses) and the resultant difficulty in trusting one another, especially those from different towns and villages, these defensive moves indicated that there were forms of re-establishing some degree of trust among them – and even between them and me.

Conclusion: "the super[market] became an army base!"

In fall 2015, right-wing Israelis and government officials made a series of visits to the Al Aqsa/Temple Mount compound in Jerusalem, and statements about those visits, which suggested Israeli moves to change the status quo at the site in favour of imposing fuller Israeli control there. With tensions still fresh from the 2014 Gaza war and related escalations of violence in the West Bank and Jerusalem, these moves sparked a spate of low-level Palestinian attacks around the country – mostly stabbings carried out by young men who acted alone, even as they were often retroactively praised by militant groups. In this context, a number of violent incidents began occurring near and even inside Israeli supermarkets that employ Palestinians, both in the West Bank and inside Israel, consisting mostly of Palestinian knife attacks as well as at least one shooting attack against Israelis. Consideration of such episodes brings to a head my argument about a tension in Israeli security between effects of normalising Israeli power and the limits of this normalisation, between Super-Israel as a civilian space and as part of a landscape of military occupation and settler-indigenous antagonism.

In one incident at a store like Super-Israel, a Palestinian from a nearby town stabbed a Jewish-Israeli settler-customer in the parking lot. Workers from that store told me that an off-duty member of the Israeli security forces who was shopping there, and apparently carrying his pistol, stepped in to shoot the Palestinian in an extremity, while an Israeli deputy manager at the store helped detain the Palestinian.[10] Then, apparently, the store flooded with Israeli security forces. As one worker at the store who I interviewed put it, "there were all kinds of military: police, army, special forces, *shabak* . . . the super[market] became an army base! [Ar. *as-suber sar mo'askar jeish*]"

Here was a more blatant manifestation of the continuity between these various military, police and private civilian security forces, as more militarised aspects of Israeli security that otherwise remained latent became activated. If Palestinians at other times expressed open-ended suspicion ("I'm telling you, the managers and *shabak* work together" or "I'm telling you, the customers know Arabic"), here one of them could make the colourful, descriptive statement that all these forces had literally been in the store, transforming it into something like a military base.

Indeed, this shift was unforgettable, in a bad way, for Palestinian workers. In such incidents, the *shabak* practices of detainment and interrogation that generally stayed outside of retail stores erupted within them. Palestinian workers with no role in such attacks could be taken to police stations and detained for days, or even detained and interrogated inside their stores. In one case I heard of, Palestinian workers were not allowed to eat, go to the bathroom, or talk on the phone for several hours, while the *shabak* interrogated them and allowed Jewish-Israelis to leave as soon as they confirmed they were Jewish. Describing such a scene, one interviewee said, "Do you see the racism [*unsuriyye*]?" Indeed the "super" could become not only a military base, but a makeshift detention centre, mirroring the Israeli regime's larger-scale forms of confining West Bank Palestinians and some Jerusalemites to enclaves behind walls and checkpoints (Weizman 2007; Gordon 2008; Khalili 2012).

Incidents like this not only heightened Palestinians' experience of the inseparability of market relations from military ones. Like the brazen Israeli performances noted earlier, but to a far greater extent, these actualisations of violence and the responses they elicited went further, undermining the normalisation of life in the settlement for Israelis themselves. For the inseparability of Palestinian as worker and threat – and at times a near-total shift to the Palestinian worker as threat – paralleled an inseparability between Israeli as customer/manager and settler or security personnel. Insofar as the mechanisms of Israeli security, reaction and escalation actively anticipated Palestinian violence and structured everyday life around its potentiality, in addition to reacting to it extensively after it happened, these security concerns were an essential part of settler market practices, far beyond these isolated incidents.

For example, after one such incident at the Super-Israel where I worked, it was both the idea of Israelis as mere customers and the physical presence of Israeli customers, that vanished: during the incident, customers had fled the store, leaving shopping carts sitting full in the aisles, with commodities strewn about and blood on the floor; and many of the customers did not return for weeks, or at all. Again, it may have been a low-level Palestinian act of violence that was a major factor in making this happen (though Palestinians and rights advocates often disputed such claims, pointing to the targeting of Palestinians who posed no immediate threat to Israelis). But the discomfort and anxiety that made many Israelis not return for weeks after this incident was already latent in everyday life. Moreover, the overwhelming security response and ensuing Israeli media coverage that sensationalised scenes of empty supermarkets also did their part in keeping customers away once they had left. Still, customers mostly seemed to come back eventually, as a fragile normalcy was gradually re-established. The supermarket's status as militarised space was dialled back, and military/civilian blurring eased back from its eruptive mode to its subtler everyday forms.[11]

Attention to how these multiple forms of security blur and otherwise relate to one another can enrich the grounds for critical comparisons between Israel/Palestine and other contemporary sites of security and militarism. For these comparisons, especially in the wake of the U.S.-led "War on Terror" and heightened Israeli counter-insurgency in the early 2000s, have often privileged Israeli military technologies and strategies, from checkpoints to forms of confinement and urban counter-insurgency (Gregory 2004; Khalili 2012). There are very good reasons for highlighting these extreme forms of occupation and violence. Still, attending further to the ways in which militarised forms of Israeli security articulate with the mundane, civilian aspects of settlement in the West Bank – including spaces such as supermarkets and the forms of security they entail – helps us account for multiple elements of the Israeli project, including its distinct configurations of settler colonialism, liberalism and neoliberalism (cf. Abu El-Haj 2010; Robinson 2013; Clarno 2017). Moreover, this attention to multiple forms of security, and multiple aspects of the Israeli colonial project, suggests broader comparisons of Israel/Palestine not only to recent sites of military occupation, such as Iraq and Afghanistan, but to other settler societies and other advanced capitalist societies, where the blurring of multiple forms of security points to broader, diverse configurations of militarised state coercion with liberal forms of politics and political economy.

Notes

1   I have anonymized all names and the name of the settlement, per IRB procedure. "Super" is an Israeli shorthand for a supermarket, and common prefix in Israeli retail store brand names, and so the pseudonym Super-Israel gets at both the corporate ("Super") and settler-nationalist ("Israel") aspects of the supermarket. Super-Israel implies a focus on Zionist/Israeli politics in its "super" as in supermarket form (not its "super" as in extra-powerful form).
2   Where it is not otherwise made clear in the text, I indicate translations to or from Hebrew with the abbreviation "Heb." and those to or from Arabic with the abbreviation "Ar." Otherwise readers can assume that most words associated with the supermarket, or spoken by Jewish-Israelis, are in Hebrew and that most speech by Palestinians is in Arabic, though there are some exceptions.
3   In this sense, I elaborate on what Grassiani and Volinz (2016) characterise as the varying levels of visibility that Israeli private security apparatuses can have for different audiences within the same space.

4 Here I adapt Joseph Masco's characterisation of U.S. national security affect as having a "circuit of shock, terror and normalization" (2014).
5 While significant access would have been possible as an American Jew, the specific access to the store as a worker was made possible by an Israeli ID which I had been pressured by the government to take as a young adult. Very early on, I explained this situation to the Palestinian workers, including that I had neither grown up in Israel nor served in the army.
6 Yellow-plated cars can be driven by Israeli citizens, Western tourists or Palestinian permanent residents of Israel – anyone but West Bank Palestinians (Bornstein 2002; Bishara 2015).
7 The Civil Administration handles the administrative aspects of Israel's occupation, such as distributing work and building permits for Palestinians. In areas under nominal Palestinian Authority (PA) control since the Oslo Accords (Areas A and B), the Civil Administration coordinates with the Palestinian Authority on such matters, a process which critics refer to as the sub-contraction of the occupation to the PA (see, e.g., Gordon 2008).
8 The prospect of the ethnographer as spy can take various forms (Verdery 2014; Johnson 2016), including those related to the ethnographer's positioning within a colonial apparatus (Deloria 1988; Marcus and Clifford 2010).
9 This was one of the many names the Palestinians called me, due in part to their difficulty in pronouncing my name, and no doubt also a way of playing with my difference.
10 More typically in such incidents at the time, on both sides of the Green Line, off-duty officers would "shoot to kill" and often did kill their targets. They sometimes did so even when, as many observers concluded, the Palestinian in question did not pose an "imminent threat of death or serious bodily injury" at the time they were killed (Human Rights Watch 2017; cf. B'Tselem 2015).
11 I borrow here from Azoulay and Ophir's (2012) similar usage of the term "eruptive", to conceptualise particular aspects of the Israeli occupation's violence, as opposed to "withheld" forms of violence.

References

Abu El-Haj, Nadia. 2010. "Racial Palestinianization and the Janus-Faced Nature of the Israeli State". *Patterns of Prejudice* 44 (1): 27–41.
Azoulay, Ariella, and Adi Ophir. 2012. *The One-State Condition: Occupation and Democracy in Israel/Palestine.* Redwood City: Stanford University Press.
Bachmann, Jan, Colleen Bell, and Caroline Holmqvist, eds. 2014. *War, Police and Assemblages of Intervention.* New York: Routledge.
Berda, Yael. 2017. *Living Emergency: Israel's Permit Regime in the Occupied West Bank.* Redwood City: Stanford University Press.
Bishara, Amahl. 2015. "Driving While Palestinian in Israel and the West Bank: The Politics of Disorientation and the Routes of a Subaltern Knowledge". *American Ethnologist* 42 (1): 33–54.
Bornstein, Avram S. 2002. "Borders and the Utility of Violence: State Effects on the "Superexploitation" of West Bank Palestinians". *Critique of Anthropology* 22 (2): 201–220.
B'Tselem. 2015. "Your Responsibility for Permitting a de Facto Death Penalty". November 25, 2015. www.btselem.org/download/20151125_letter_to_pm_on_extrajudicial_killings_eng.pdf.

Camp, Jordan T., and Christina Heatherton, eds. 2016. *Policing the Planet: Why the Policing Crisis Led to Black Lives Matter*. New York: Verso.

Clarno, Andy. 2017. Neoliberal Apartheid: Palestine/Israel and South Africa after 1994. Chicago: University of Chicago Press.

Duffield, Mark. 2001. *Global Governance and the New Wars: The Merging of Development and Security*. New York: Zed Books.

Fanon, Frantz. 2004. *The Wretched of the Earth*. Translated by Richard Philcox. New York: Grove Press.

Feldman, Ilana. 2015. *Police Encounters: Security and Surveillance in Gaza Under Egyptian Rule*. Redwood City: Stanford University Press.

Goffman, Erving. 1981. *Forms of Talk*. Philadelphia, PA: University of Pennsylvania Press.

Goldstein, Daniel M. 2012. *Outlawed: Between Security and Rights in a Bolivian City*. Durham: Duke University Press Books.

Gordon, Neve. 2008. *Israel's Occupation*. Berkeley: University of California Press.

Grassiani, Erella, and Lior Volinz. 2016. "Intimidation, Reassurance, and Invisibility: Israeli Security Agents in the Old City of Jerusalem". *Focaal* 2016 (75).

Gregory, Derek. 2004. *The Colonial Present: Afghanistan, Palestine, and Iraq*. Malden: Blackwell Publishing.

Hall, Kathleen. 2012. "Security and the Neoliberal State: British Political Imaginaries After 7/7". In *Ethnographies of Neoliberalism*, edited by Carol J. Greenhouse, 13–27. Philadelphia: University of Pennsylvania Press.

Human Rights Watch. 2017. "Israel/Palestine: Some Officials Backing 'Shoot-to-Kill': Calls for Extrajudicial Killings of Palestinian Suspects Proliferate". www.hrw.org/news/2017/01/02/israel/palestine-some-officials-backing-shoot-kill.

Jauregui, Beatrice. 2010. "Bluing Green in the Maldives: Countering Citizen Insurgency by 'Civil'-Izing National Security". In *Anthropology and Global Counterinsurgency*, edited by John D. Kelly, Beatrice Jauregui, Sean T. Mitchell, and Jeremy Walton. Chicago: University of Chicago Press.

Kadman, Noga. 2012. *Employment of Palestinians in Israel and the Settlements: Restrictive Policies and Abuse of Rights*. Tel Aviv: Kav LaOved.

Kelly, John D., Beatrice Jauregui, Sean T. Mitchell, and Jeremy Walton, eds. 2010. *Anthropology and Global Counterinsurgency*. Chicago: University of Chicago Press.

Kelly, Tobias. 2009. *Law, Violence and Sovereignty Among West Bank Palestinians*. New York: Cambridge University Press.

Kershner, Isabel. 2015. "West Bank Shopping Complex, a Symbol of Coexistence, Is Shaken". *New York Times*, December 14, 2015. www.nytimes.com/2015/12/15/world/middleeast/west-bank-shopping-complex-a-symbol-of-coexistence-is-shaken.html.

Khalili, Laleh. 2012. *Time in the Shadows: Confinement in Counterinsurgencies*. Redwood City: Stanford University Press.

Lakoff, Andrew. 2008. "The Generic Biothreat, Or, How We Became Unprepared". *Cultural Anthropology* 23 (3): 399–428.

Lutz, Catherine A. 2002. *Homefront: A Military City and the American Twentieth Century*. Boston: Beacon Press.

Masco, Joseph. 2014. *The Theater of Operations: National Security Affect From the Cold War to the War on Terror*. Durham: Duke University Press.

O'Neill, Kevin Lewis. 2015. *Secure the Soul: Christian Piety and Gang Prevention in Guatemala*. Oakland: University of California Press.

Rana, Aziz. 2014. "Settler Wars and the National Security State". *Settler Colonial Studies* 4 (2): 171–175.

Robinson, Shira. 2013. *Citizen Strangers: Palestinians and the Birth of Israel's Liberal Settler State*. Stanford: Stanford University Press.

Salamanca, Omar Jabary, et al. 2012. "Past Is Present: Settler Colonialism in Palestine". *Settler Colonial Studies* 2 (1): 1–8.

Schmitt, Carl. 2007. *The Concept of the Political*. Chicago: The University of Chicago Press.

Taussig, Michael. 1999. *Defacement: Public Secrecy and the Labor of the Negative*. Stanford: Stanford University Press.

Weizman, Eyal. 2007. *Hollow Land: Israel's Architecture of Occupation*. New York: Verso.

2 Security blurs in Haiti

Urban armed groups as providers of (in)security

Moritz Schuberth

Introduction

The traditional Weberian understanding of the state as the sole provider of security is inconsistent with numerous empirical cases of "oligopolies of violence", which "comprise a fluctuating number of partly competing, partly co-operating actors of violence of different quality" (Mehler 2004, 539). This is especially true in so-called fragile and conflict-affected states (FCAS), which are characterised by the proliferation of non-state armed groups (NSAGs) that are not only causing insecurity, but have also taken over state security functions (Andersen et al. 2007). These diverse trends challenge traditional notions of security, which distinguish sharply between formal and informal dimensions of security, between state and non-state security providers and between providers of security and providers of insecurity. Nevertheless, numerous academics and practitioners alike continue to frame security governance in fragile and conflict-affected states through stringent analytical categories that are far removed from the blurriness of security actors in these settings. The notion of *security blurs*, which depicts the intersection of formal and informal, legal and illegal, as well as state and non-state dimensions of security governance, appears thus more analytically useful to make sense of the plethora of actors involved in the co-production of (in)security.

Based on empirical evidence from the informal settlements of Haiti's capital Port-au-Prince, this chapter challenges traditional understandings of security governance by focusing on *security blurs*, and specifically on the blurring between providers of security and providers of insecurity. More precisely, I argue that one and the same group can be both a source of security and a source of insecurity for the community in which they are nested, depending primarily on the constantly shifting interests of their external sponsors. Categorising these groups as militias, gangs or vigilantes – as is still commonly done by researchers and practitioners on the ground – can thus provide only a limited snapshot of the dominant function they fulfil at a given point in time.

The argument brought forward in this chapter is informed by empirical evidence gathered during a period of six months of fieldwork in Port-au-Prince from June to December 2013. I conducted 37 interviews primarily with international agencies,[1] but also with community leaders, religious leaders, local NGOs, CSOs, peace initiatives and current and former members of urban armed groups (UAGs).[2] To increase the validity of my research, I triangulated the data by carrying out observations within informal settlements in Port-au-Prince between June and December 2013. However, access to certain areas in Cité Soleil was more restricted from October 2013 onwards due to increasing incidents of fighting between UAGs and police and between different UAGs themselves.

After introducing the predominant analytical lenses – state fragility, patronage and criminality – through which urban, armed groups in Haiti tend to be framed in the academic literature, I will discuss their emergence and their role in Haiti's contemporary history. Subsequently, to move beyond the dichotomies of informal/formal or state/non-state provision of security/insecurity, I will apply the concept of security blurs to show that there is no clear distinction between providers of security and providers of insecurity in Haiti. Lastly, in order to disentangle the processes that lead to the blurring of security in Haiti, I will shift the focus on sponsors rather than producers of (in)security by way of discussing the internal and external functions which urban armed groups fulfil on behalf of their members, politico-criminal sponsors, or the community in which they are nested.

The framing of urban armed groups (UAGs) in Haiti

Even though there are notable exceptions, an important part of the literature on Haiti frames UAGs in the country through one of several specific analytical lenses.[3] As illustrated in Table 2.1, each analytical lens emphasises another function the UAG in question fulfils for one of its stakeholders (Schuberth 2016a). First of all, when a UAG is analysed through the framework of state failure, the security dimension is highlighted, and the group is likely to be portrayed as a vigilante group providing security for their community. Second, when a UAG is analysed through the framework of patronage, the political dimension is underlined, and the group is most likely described as a militia working on behest of political sponsors paying for their violent services. Third and lastly, when a UAG is analysed through the framework of criminality and delinquency, the economic dimension is

Table 2.1 Functions and stakeholders of different ideal types of UAGs

Type of UAG	Dominant Function	Key Stakeholder	Analytical Frame
Vigilantes	Security	Community	State Fragility
Militias	Political	Political Sponsors	Patronage/Clientelism
Gangs	Economic	Criminal Sponsors	Criminality

emphasised, and the group is probably depicted as a criminal gang pursuing the economic interests of its criminal sponsors (Schuberth 2015a). As the following paragraphs will reveal, the three different explanatory frames are clearly visible in the literature on Haiti and have been equally evident throughout the interviews I conducted in Haiti.

Haiti being seen as an archetypical "failed state", entire monographs have been dedicated to analysing the country's troubled history and contemporary conflicts through the lens of state fragility (Gros 2012). From this point of view, UAGs in Haiti are seen as crime-control vigilantes or self-defence forces filling the gap of security provision that has been left by an absent state. According to Kivland (2014, 678), for instance, leaders of UAGs "'make the state' by performing its work and [. . .] see themselves less as resisting state authority than as furnishing state-like community and connections by providing security against outside threats". Likewise, a number of practitioners on the ground have adopted the frame of state fragility. For instance, Chilean Brigadier General Eduardo Aldunate Herman (2010, 107, 110), former Deputy Commander of MINUSTAH, recalls that "[d]uring my posting, the absence of the state there was complete. The strongest criminal gangs fought constantly among themselves for turf. [. . .] On that turf, there was no rule of law".

The role of patronage is the second frame through which a number of authors have analysed the roots of political conflict in Haiti (Peirce 2007; Lunde 2012). From this point of view, UAGs emerged as part of the pro-democracy movement during the Duvalier dictatorships and formed the basis of Arsitide's *Lavalas* party, for which they acted as distributors of patronage to popular neighbourhoods in exchange for political support (Muggah 2013). For example, Perito and Dziedzic (2008, 2) explain that "powerful elites from [. . .] Aristide to the bourgeoisie, exploited gangs as instruments of political warfare, providing arms, funding and protection from arrest". Hence, when analysed through the explanatory frame of patronage and clientelism, Haiti's UAGs are seen as popular militias instrumentalised by political entrepreneurs.

The third frame through which UAGs in Haiti are frequently analysed is that of criminality and delinquency (Cockayne 2009). By way of example, Kemp et al. (2013, 34) attribute the rise of insecurity in Port-au-Prince to UAGs "many of whom were heavily involved in illicit activities [and] also developed links with drug traffickers". Status-seeking behaviour is seen as equally important as economic incentives to explain the criminal behaviour of Haiti's UAGs (Hammond 2012, 19). In line with this, a number of studies have highlighted the impact of cultural and societal influences on the delinquent behaviour of juvenile gang members in Haiti's popular neighbourhoods (Willman and Marcelin 2010). Thus, seen through the frame of criminality, UAGs in Haiti combine the economic dimension of criminal gangs and aspects of delinquency typically associated with unsupervised youth groups.

However, factions of Haiti's elite also misused the framing of UAGs as purely predatory and criminal groups in order to indiscriminately criminalise Aristide supporters or generally all residents of popular neighbourhoods (Nicolas 2006, 187). This misuse of the lens of criminality for political purposes shows the limits and dangers of analysing complex actors involved in the co-production of security blurs through simplistic frames such as state fragility, patronage, or criminality – a practice that is still prevalent in much of the literature on Haiti, as this section has shown. As the following section will reveal, UAGs in Haiti are a multidimensional phenomenon whose emergence can be traced back to a mix of institutional fragility, political mobilisation, and self-interested motifs (Schuberth 2017b).

The emergence of urban armed groups (UAGs) in Haiti

The use of non-state armed groups (NSAGs) by those in power to impose order and intimidate the opposition is not a new phenomenon in Haiti's history. Faustin Soulouque used his *zinglins*, or political thugs, as early as in the mid-19th century (Nicolas 2006, 187). More than a century later, but inspired by Soulouque, François Duvalier's rule relied heavily on the use of an oppressive paramilitary force in the form of *Tonton Macoutes* (Diederich and Burt 2005). In the post-Duvalier and pre-Aristide period, Duvalierist elements equally resorted to the violence of ex-military and former *Macoutes* (Fatton Jr. 2002). Yet, the most infamous example of the instrumentalisation of NSAGs – in this case, urban armed groups (UAGs) based in Port-au-Prince's informal settlements – occurred during the rule of Jean-Bertrand Aristide. Aristide had become the country's first democratically elected President in 1991, five years after a popular uprising had ended the dynastic dictatorship of François "Papa Doc" Duvalier and his son Jean-Claude "Baby Doc" (Fatton Jr. 2007).

The origins of Haiti's contemporary UAGs can be traced back to neighbourhood organisations which had emerged as "pockets of tacit resistance" to the Duvalier dictatorship, ultimately leading to the fall of Jean-Claude Duvalier in 1986 (Muggah 2013, 301; Kivland 2014, 677). Yet, far from constituting a peaceful grassroots movement, the groups aimed for the violent "*dechoukaj*" or uprooting of Duvalierism (Aristide and Richardson 1995, 183). This entailed not only the overthrow of Duvalier himself, but also the seeking revenge against everyone linked to his dictatorial rule, most notably his *Tonton Macoutes* (Jean and Maesschalck 1999, 46f). Among the neighbourhood organisations involved in the *dechoukaj* were *brigades de vigilance* or vigilante committees, which had been formed in the run-up to the 1987 elections in order to "protect the electoral offices, the ballots and the volunteers who were helping to organize the elections locally" (Wilentz 1989, 301).

After the elections, the *brigades* continued to fulfil various purposes. Internally, they acted as informal crime-control groups in marginalised neighbourhoods lacking state security provision; however, they have been found to occasionally join forces with criminal elements (Kovats-Bernat 2006, 88). Externally, they protected their community against attacks from Duvalierist elements and oppressive state security forces after the military-led coup d'état against Aristide in 1991 (Hallward 2007, 139). Despite their resort to "popular justice" – for instance pillaging and setting on fire hotels that were suspected to serve as a hiding space for criminals – they could continue to count on the support of their ousted leader, Aristide, to whom they were linked through the *Fanmi Lavalas* movement (Aristide and Richardson 1995, 182).

Aristide's first presidency was cut short after eight months by a military coup d'état led by General Raoul Cédras, who presided over a regime of terror until Aristide was reinstated by the U.S.-led *Operation Uphold Democracy* in 1994 (Fatton Jr. 2002). After his re-election in 2000, parts of the Haitian army that Aristide had disbanded in 1995 started a paramilitary campaign to oust the newly elected president (Sprague 2012). In the face of armed domestic opposition and a lack of external support amidst allegations of electoral fraud, widespread corruption, and involvement in drug trafficking, Aristide tried to consolidate his rule with the help of UAGs also known as *baz* (Fleurimond 2009). He did so by expanding his clientelistic network – the *organisations populaires* – while arming their criminal wing – the *chimères* – as a powerful irregular force to silence the opposition (Dupuy 2007). Yet, he soon lost control over the Pandora's Box he had opened. In 2004, an unlikely alliance of rural paramilitaries and factions of the UAGs that had formerly constituted his support base forced Aristide out of power by (Fatton Jr. 2006, 124).

Security blurs in Haiti: urban armed groups (UAGs) as providers of (in)security

As the preceding section revealed, UAGs in Port-au-Prince have been both the source of security and the source of insecurity throughout contemporary Haitian history (Schuberth 2017a).[4] Indeed, the fact that Haiti's UAGs have multiple dimensions has been acknowledged to a certain degree in the literature and by practitioners alike. For instance, Marcelin (2015, 234) notes that Haiti's popular neighbourhoods are "a site of resistance and struggle where criminality and politics intersect", while Di Razza (2010, 54) confirms that the activities of UAGs located in these areas "oscillate, in an often ambiguous manner, between political struggle, popular defence, and criminality".[5]

Likewise, a number of respondents with close contact to UAGs underlined the fluidity and blurriness between the different analytical categories. According to the Security Coordinator of the Brazilian NGO Viva Rio, which has a strong presence in the low-income neighbourhood of Bel Air, "there's a social aspect, a political aspect, and then there's armed violence. Within a sole *baz*, you can find these three groups. And it's difficult to find a *baz* that doesn't combine these three elements".[6] Likewise, Viva Rio's Liaison Officer distinguished between three categories of UAGs in Haiti:

> First, you have militants, people who are involved in politics. Then we identified the gangs. And we identified mercenaries. [. . .] Sometimes the militants are paid and they become mercenaries, sometimes militants are linked to the gangs. They resemble each other. It's not always possible to identify who are the mercenaries, who are the militants, who are the gangs. [. . .] One moment they are militants, the next moment they are gangs, and another moment they are mercenaries. Often they use the cover of "*organisations populaires*", but they are involved in activities of banditry. [. . .] The gangs hide behind the militants. As I said, there's political violence and social violence, so it's easy to hide social violence behind the militants. That way, they commit violence, banditry, but they have no real needs.[7]

Moreover, widely differing perspectives on UAGs in Haiti can even be found within one and the same organisation (Schuberth 2016b). For instance, a U.S. subcontractor managing grants for a major donor with only limited exposure to the communities in question gave a rather idealistic view of UAGs as respected community organisations headed by notable leaders to which "everyone in the community looks up to".[8] This interpretation is in stark contrast to that given by a Haitian respondent who had actually implemented projects for the same organisation on the ground, recalling long and rather frightening negotiations about access with armed leaders of UAGs at night, where having a loaded gun pointed to their head for the entire meeting was the norm rather than the exception.[9] Ultimately, as most UAGs in Haiti combine political, criminal and security-related aspects, the term used to describe them might reveal more about the person using the term than about the actual nature of the groups themselves (Schuberth 2018a).

Given the fluidity and blurriness between the provision of security and the provision of insecurity by UAGs, they might as well be reframed as providers of (in)security. Building on Elwert (1999) and Mehler (2004), providers of (in)security can be defined as violent entrepreneurs serving the market of (in)security in areas where security governance is characterised by an oligopoly rather than a monopoly of violence.[10] The market of (in)security can be seen a specific section of the market of violence, defined by Elwert (2003, 25) as "a field of activity which is mainly characterised by economic aims, in which both robbery and barter and the related activities of collection of ransoms, protection money, road tolls etc. feature". Providers of (in)security are willing to provide whatever good – security or insecurity – the highest bidder currently demands. Whether armed violence is employed to advance security or insecurity therefore depends on the preference of the sponsors.

This chapter hence argues that the motivation of those *committing* acts of armed violence remains the same, whereas the often-overlapping criminal and political priorities of those *commissioning* these acts are constantly shifting. The following sections suggest two conceptual adjustments in order to improve our understanding of the blurred lines between the provision of security and the provision of insecurity. First, it is suggested to shift the focus of analysis from the producers to the sponsors of violence. Second, it is suggested to overcome the analytical divide between vigilantes providing security on one hand, and militias or gangs causing insecurity on the other hand.

Given significant structural constraints in Port-au-Prince's poor neighbourhoods, UAGs have the internal function of generating income for their members, whereas their external function can change between providing security for their community and providing insecurity for their criminal or political patrons. The main sponsors of UAGs throughout Haiti's recent history have been various political actors. During periods of decreasing demand for their violent service by politicians, however, UAGs appear to resort to two alternative sources of income: either they increase their collaboration with organised crime groups, or they extract resources from their own communities. Thus, while UAGs remain driven by the incentive to gain income by whatever means, external interests can implicate them in power politics or organised criminal activities.

Internal and external functions of providers of (in)security

Depending on the preference of the highest bidder in the market of (in)security, UAGs resort to the use of armed violence in order to provide either security or insecurity. However, the majority of studies on UAGs in Haiti and elsewhere focus on the motivation of *perpetrators* of violence and not on that of their *sponsors*. It is commonly taken as a given that "a perpetrator's motivations" are the decisive factor when classifying "an act of armed violence [as] politically or economically motivated" (del Frate and De Martino 2013, 9). This perspective presupposes that members of UAGs make the deliberate choice of whether to engage in violence to protect and maintain order in their community or to do so for the political and profit-oriented aims of their sponsors. Yet, looking at the motivation of those who commit violent acts fails to adequately take into account the impact of structural constraints and external interests.

Those living outside and those living within deprived communities seem to agree that the range of options available to members of UAGs is limited. In the opinion of a representative of the UN, "gangs are [. . .] not to be looked at as the cause of violence, the cause of problems. They are the result of structural problems".[11] Likewise, a former UAG member explains that "they don't have any means, they are frustrated, it's easy to manipulate them. [. . .] It's easy to use a *baz* to commit crimes".[12] Thus, a number of respondents confirmed that grievances are so pressing in Haiti's slums that the mostly juvenile members of UAGs are primarily driven by income-generating and status-seeking activities.

Of course, most youth growing up in such conditions do not join UAGs, so this is not their inevitable fate. But those who do join such groups are, from the point of view of a humanitarian worker who tried to educate gang members in the principles of international humanitarian law, "mainly motivated by money. [. . .] Some of the gang leaders, they are very, very young. So if you talk with them about politics, they don't know anything about politics. Politics is money".[13] The director of *Lakou Lapè*, a local peace building agency, confirmed that "they are not necessarily politically motivated based on philosophy or anything like that. Most of them are there for the bucks, for making dollars".[14]

This chapter suggests shifting the focus of analysis from the *producers* to the *sponsors* of violence. Drawing on Gambetta's (1996) and Volkov's (2002) work on the Italian and Russian Mafia, members of UAGs can be seen as profit-oriented violent entrepreneurs who are seeking to improve their limited life chances by way of offering their violent services on the market of (in)security, regardless of whether they serve the security-related interests of their community or their politico-criminal sponsors' interest in insecurity. In this respect, whether UAGs provide security or cause insecurity depends not on their members who *commit* the violence, but on the sponsors who *commission* it. Thus, it is important to distinguish between internal and external functions of UAGs in Haiti.

Internally, UAGs function as "potential forms of asset building and accumulation" for their members (Rodgers 2007, 180). The external function, by contrast, depends on the demands of the patron (Schuberth 2018b). From this perspective, UAGs whose members are consistently driven by economic incentives can be paid to cause insecurity, which might have a political or economic function for their sponsor. In the absence of patrons, UAGs turn towards their community to generate income; that is, they turn into a protection racket. Consequently, it appears crucial to focus on the role of patrons who "hire" the violent services of UAGs in order to better understand the co-production of (in)security. Patrons are usually part of Haiti's political and economic elite, whereas members of the UAGs they utilise belong to the country's most deprived social stratum. In this respect, a MINUSTAH official explains that:

> The Haitian bourgeoisie pays these groups to protect themselves [. . .] and at the same time you have the conflict between politicians who also pay these groups, so it's exploding now. The Haitian bourgeoisie is not innocent regarding the gang problem.[15]

That being said, it is not always easy to draw a clear-cut distinction between patrons and clients. UAGs in Haiti typically have between 30 and 50 members or affiliates, the majority of whom are unarmed juveniles. On top of the hierarchy are the leader and his two or three "lieutenants" who are often heavily armed and pocket the vast bulk of profits from any operations. It is possible for the leader to ascend towards the status of a patron, residing outside of the slum in which his UAG is located and outsourcing the day-to-day business to his lieutenants. Such upward climbers might eventually hold political or administrative jobs at the municipal or even national level.[16]

Likewise, the distinction between political and criminal patrons is not always that straightforward. There are not only personal and familial relationships between politicians and organised criminals, but top public office-holders have repeatedly been involved in transnational criminal activities, while certain politicians once started their career as gang leaders.[17] Hence, some patrons are pursuing politico-criminal interests, the priority of which tends to swing toward the political during election periods and toward the criminal in between elections. In such cases, it is difficult to even distinguish between the political sphere and the criminal sphere, as political power begets economic power, and economic power begets political power (Schuberth 2015b).

The extent to which different patrons have an impact on a particular UAG at a given point in time depends on both temporal and geographical factors. Emphasising temporal variations in external drivers of conflict, a regional coordinator for MINUSTAH explains that "when elections are approaching, [conflicts] will intensify. That's why there are currently many power struggles, [because] every group is trying to position itself".[18] At the same time, a security coordinator with Viva Rio stresses the importance of geographical proximity to potential sponsors:

> Communities which are close to the market use the market. Communities which are close to the national palace use politics. And communities which are neither close to the market nor to the national palace, but which are "ghetto", very isolated, without roads, they produce [. . .] a very violent gang.[19]

During election periods, the demand of political actors for the violent service of UAGs rises. Likewise, when the political environment and the climate of insecurity are particularly conducive for large-scale criminal activities, organised crime groups engage UAGs to carry out kidnappings and the like. Lastly, the absence of external patrons pushes formerly sponsored UAGs to increase the revenue extracted from their own or neighbouring communities; hence they demand money from residents and businesses in their turf for the provision of security. The following sections provide a more detailed account of the processes behind the production of security and insecurity by Haiti's UAGs by examining their relationship to politics, to organised crime and to their community.

UAGs as providers of insecurity

In some parts of Port-au-Prince, the patron-client relationship between political sponsors and UAGs is based on historically well-established ties. In the low-income neighbourhood of Bel Air, for instance, Aristide nurtured his ties to UAGs by distributing funds from state-owned companies to their members who received "salaries" without actually working there.[20] In exchange for their violent services, the armed wing of these groups received financial support, arms and protection from being arrested by police (Dupuy 2007). As a demobilised UAG member recounts:

> The *baz*, they wanted money, but they didn't want to work. That's a problem. Aristide said: "you will work at TELECO; you will work at PEN; and you will work at EDH". So all *baz* members had a job, but they were only hanging around, drinking and smoking all day because they received money [anyways]. In the end, they also became armed for Aristide. *Baz* members were saying, "I have my arm to protect the power of Aristide".[21]

However, it has to be stressed that a wide range of political actors in Haiti uses such methods and that UAGs have repeatedly switched from one political side to the other, depending on which party remunerates them most generously. In this respect, Mobekk (2008, 116) points out that "[p]olitical groups of all shades used the disenfranchised and poor youths to further their own agendas", while a Haitian humanitarian worker confirms that gangs are "used as tools to carry out some work, I mean some dirty work".[22] A UAG member explained to me that

> Bel Air is the *baz* of Aristide. And when elections are approaching and another candidate wants to enter Bel Air, this will pose a problem; this will cause violence because it's already conquered. But in other cases, the *baz* are used by numerous politicians. That's why I'm telling you that there is no fidelity.[23]

On top of that, it is widely acknowledged that the long-delayed elections were behind an upsurge of turf wars in Cité Soleil in the last quarter of 2013.[24] As a humanitarian worker commented

> But now what is going on in Cité Soleil is really highly politically marked. Because there will be elections in 2014 in the communes and Cité Soleil is one of them. And they are fighting in the perspective of gaining the commune.[25]

Lavalas, the historical ally of UAGs, was trying to regain its influence in Cité Soleil.[26] At the same time, the then-President Martelly was trying to buy the support of UAGs, with whom he has no historical ties and which he could not control solely by force. Towards the end of 2013, this proxy fighting for political influence culminated in the burning and decapitation of members of rival UAGs.[27] As a former social mobilisation consultant for UN-Habitat sums it up:

> In Haiti, if you want to have power, you have to control the popular neighbourhoods. So if you want to control the popular neighbourhoods,

[. . .] you have to pay the bandits. [. . .] The people changed, but it's the same methodology. What I cannot control by force, I control by money.[28]

After the ouster of Aristide in 2004, patronage in the form of monthly payments for members of UAGs on the payroll of state-owned companies ceased to flow (Dupuy 2005). Moreover, around 750 police officers associated with the ousted president were fired without being disarmed (Lunde 2012). This left a large number of armed, unemployed young men without regular income two alternatives to make quick money: working for organised crime groups, or extracting protection money from their community. One task for which organised crime groups have "subcontracted" UAGs is kidnapping.

According to the International Crisis Group (2006), organised criminal groups had become the new patrons of UAGs, and kidnappings served their vested interest to politically destabilise the country. Up to today, the most important sponsors of kidnappings in Haiti appear to belong to the country's economic elite, parts of which are engaged in organised criminal activities in addition to their legal business operations. Some members of the Haitian business class have been found to subcontract UAGs through a network of intermediaries, in which police officers often assume the role of middlemen.[29] As a former social mobilisation consultant for UN-Habitat told me, "all the businesses are controlled by a few families, mafias one could say. And these mafias have links to armed groups, which are based in poor neighbourhoods. It's a manipulation from top to bottom".[30]

In some cases, members of UAGs are hired for legal activities, such as providing security for factories, which are located within or in close proximity to gang-controlled areas.[31] In other cases, the nature of their cooperation is illegal and its purpose is to provide insecurity. The best-documented example in this respect is the kidnapping ring led by Clifford Brandt, a member of one of the richest and most influential families in Haiti. This "family clan gang",[32] as a MINUSTAH official called it, ordered kidnappings of family members of business rivals, in addition to being engaged in money laundering and arms trafficking. With Brandt having links to former President Martelly's family, Haitian authorities did not properly investigate the case "until they were forced to by the U.S. Government" (Charles 2012). This points to a general collusion between politics and organised crime in Haiti, which makes it difficult to determine whether insecurity caused by UAGs serves political or economic objectives.

All things considered, the loyalty of UAGs to their political patrons depends not on political convictions, but on monetary incentives, either in the form of long-established patronage networks or through quick injections of money. During election periods, whether in 2004 or ten years later, UAGs are paid to carry out acts of armed violence that cause insecurity and advance the political power of their patrons. In between elections, UAGs are hired to provide insecurity that facilitates the conduct of organised criminal activities to increase the economic power of their patrons. Since economic and political power are so intertwined, however, one could also say that at any point in time, patrons pay UAGs to provide insecurity that advances their politico-criminal interests.

UAGs as providers of security

Apart from working on behalf of organised crime groups, extracting resources from their own or neighbouring communities has been another strategy employed by UAGs to compensate for loss of revenue when patronage from political actors diminished. Yet, this is only one aspect of the ambivalent relationship between UAGs and their own community, for whom they can be both a source of security and a source of insecurity. Mobekk and Street (2006, 3) described this ambiguous relationship as a "complex mixture of racketeering and protectionism".

On one hand, UAGs act to a certain degree as a substitute for the absent state. A UN official described the situation within informal settlements in the following terms: "[s]o you have no jobs, you have no social security, you have no infrastructure, you have no state. And if the state is present, it's seen as a negative element".[33] The negative perception of the state stems from the fact that many residents have very limited experience with authorities other than abusive encounters with police officers. One respondent noted that "if there was an efficient police force with an adequate number of officers to protect all the population, the people wouldn't find themselves in the situation of being forced to choose between the gang and the police",[34] whereas a former DDR Officer confirms that "the police are sometimes also perceived as a predator from whom one needs protection. And gangs can protect the community from penetration by the police and also from surrounding districts, because the different districts are in war with each other".[35]

In this context, UAGs provide not only security, but also other basic services such as waste disposal, payment of school fees and burial costs, and offer entertainment in the form of concerts or community parties (Kolbe 2013). As a former social mobilisation consultant for UN-Habitat told me, "when the state is not there, the armed group which controls the neighbourhood can offer jobs, can distribute money, and can send kids to school, so it's a bit like Pablo Escobar".[36] Consequently, residents have repeatedly protected UAGs against law enforcement agencies, be it because of the benefits they receive or due to fear of retaliation (Mobekk 2008).

On the other hand, especially when revenues from their sponsors are diminishing, UAGs turn towards extracting resources at the local level through protection rackets and petty crimes. A number of studies maintain that UAGs levy taxes on transportation, basic services such as water supply or medical facilities, and even on remittances from Haitians living abroad (Cockayne 2009). Thus, the rule by UAGs over their turf has been interpreted as a localised version of Tilly's (1985) model of a protection racket state (Peirce 2007), while Hammond (2012, 36) compares Haiti's UAGs to "urban warlords" who maintain themselves through the extraction of resources from residents living in the territory they control.

Concluding remarks

Drawing on the notion of security blurs, this chapter proposed two conceptual adjustments aimed at improving our understanding of the processes that led to blurred lines between the provision of security and the provision of insecurity by UAGs in Port-au-Prince. First, by way of shifting the focus of analysis from the producers to the sponsors of violence, and second, by overcoming the analytical divide between vigilantes providing security for their community on one hand, and militias or gangs causing insecurity on behalf of their politico-criminal sponsors on the other hand. Instead, it was suggested to analyse UAGs as violent entrepreneurs offering their violent services to the highest bidder on the market of (in)security.

From this perspective, the internal function of asset building and accumulations remains broadly the same for the members of UAGs, while their external function depends primarily on their sponsors. In this sense, whether UAGs provide security or insecurity depends less on the motivation of their members and more on the interests of the patron who has the largest influence on a particular group during a given period of time. It has been shown that the decreasing impact of political sponsors after a period of political turmoil surrounding the second coup d'état against Aristide in 2004 prompted UAGs to seek alternative revenue by providing security in exchange for protection fees from their communities or by providing insecurity on behalf of organised crime groups.

During election periods, however, political sponsors can reactivate the political function of UAGs, a scenario that occurred during my fieldwork in Haiti against the background of the long-delayed elections that took place eventually in the end of 2015. This means that rather than framing UAGs in Haiti as political militias, criminal gangs, or vigilantes, an explanation based on the analysis of constantly shifting priorities of often overlapping patrons seems more fruitful. The findings of this chapter could be compared to cases of providers of (in)security in other countries in the region and beyond, including Central America, Colombia and Kenya (Schuberth 2014).

Notes

1 Concern International, ICRC, IOM, International Rescue Committee, MSF, UNDP, UN-Habitat, UN OCHA, USAID, Viva Rio, as well as the civilian and military sections of MINUSTAH. All quotes in this article of interviews conducted in French or Haitian Creole were translated into English by the author.
2 In this article, I use the term UAGs to refer to all types of groups as a way of incorporating the blurriness between the different categories. In direct quotes,

I keep the label that the author or respondent used to describe UAGs, even if I do not endorse its connotation.

3 Apart from labelling Haiti's UAGs as vigilantes, militias or gangs, academic studies often use local expressions to describe UAGs – the most commonly used are *baz* ("base"), *organisations populaires* and *chimères*, which refers "both to a mythical, fire-breathing demon and the French word for a wild or upsetting dream" (Deibert 2005, 95).

4 Interviews with former UAG members and staff of international NGOs in Haiti, October and November 2013.

5 Translated from French by author.

6 Interview with Viva Rio, Pétion-Ville, October 2013.

7 Interview with Viva Rio, Pétion-Ville, October 2013.

8 Interview, Pétion-Ville, September 2013.

9 Interview, Port-au-Prince, November 2013.

10 Contrary to the concept of "security markets" (Lambach 2007), the concept of markets of (in)security contains the provision of insecurity for economic or political purposes.

11 Interview with CVR (Community Violence Reduction) section of MINUSTAH, Port-au-Prince, October 2013.

12 Interview with reintegrated gang member, Haiti, October 2013.

13 Interview with ICRC, Port-au-Prince, November 2013.

14 Interview with *Lakou Lapè*, Port-au-Prince, October 2013.

15 Interview with MINUSTAH's CVR section, Port-au-Prince, October 2013.

16 This paragraph is based on an interview with a former programme coordinator of MINUSTAH CVR, Pétion-Ville, October 2013. On the political ambitions of gang leaders, see also Neiburg et al. (2011) and Erickson (2014).

17 See also Cockayne (2009) and Kemp et al. (2013).

18 Interview with MINUSTAH's CVR section, Port-au-Prince, October 2013.

19 Interview with Viva Rio, Pétion-Ville, October 2013.

20 Interview with UAG member, Haiti, October 2013. See also Kivland (2009) and Lunde (2012).

21 Interview with reintegrated gang member, Haiti, October 2013. TELECO, PEN and EDH are state-owned enterprises in Haiti.

22 Interview with Haitian humanitarian worker, Port-au-Prince, November 2013.

23 Interview with UAG member, Haiti, October 2013.

24 Interviews with Viva Rio, UNDP, ICRC, community leaders and international experts, Haiti, September and October 2013. The elections were originally scheduled for 2011, but were postponed numerous times before they took place towards the end of 2015.

25 Interview with Haitian humanitarian worker, Port-au-Prince, November 2013.

26 Interview with community leader, Cité Soleil, October 2013.

27 Conversations with residents and community leaders, Cité Soleil, September 2013.

28 Interview with former social mobilisation consultant, Pétion-Ville, October 2013.

29 Interview with international expert, Haiti, October 2013. See also RNDDH (2012).

30 Interview with former social mobilisation consultant, Pétion-Ville, October 2013.

31 Interview with CVR section of MINUSTAH, Port-au-Prince, October 2013.

32 Interview with MINUSTAH official, Port-au-Prince, October 2013.

33 Interview with CVR section of MINUSTAH, October 2014.

34 Interview with ICRC, Port-au-Prince, November 2013.

35 Interview with former DDR Officer, Pétion-Ville, October 2013.

36 Interview with former social mobilisation consultant, Pétion-Ville, October 2013.

References

Andersen, Louise, Bjørn Møller, and Finn Stepputat. 2007. *Fragile States and Insecure People? Violence, Security, and Statehood in the Twenty-first Century.* New York and Basingstoke: Palgrave Macmillan.

Aristide, Marx V., and Laurie Richardson. 1995. "Haiti's Popular Resistance". In *Haiti: Dangerous Crossroads*, edited by Deidre Mcfadyen and Pierre Laramée, 181–194. Boston: South End Press.

Charles, Jacqueline. 2012. "Haiti Kidnapping: Shrouded in Secrecy". *Merced Sun-Star*, November 19, 2012.

Cockayne, James. 2009. "Winning Haiti's Protection Competition: Organized Crime and Peace Operations Past, Present and Future". *International Peacekeeping* 16 (1): 77–99.

Deibert, Michael. 2005. *Notes From the Last Testament: The Struggle for Haiti.* New York: Seven Stories Press.

del Frate, Anna Alvazzi, and Luigi De Martino. 2013. "Everyday Dangers: Non-conflict Armed Violence". In *Small Arms Survey 2013: Everyday Dangers*, edited by Emile Lebrun et al., 7–15. Geneva: Small Arms Survey.

Di Razza, Namie. 2010. *L'ONU en Haïti Depuis 2004: Ambitions et Déconvenues des Opérations de Paix Multidimensionnelles.* Paris: L'Harmattan.

Diederich, Bernard, and Al Burt. 2005. *Papa Doc & The Tontons Macoutes.* Princeton: Markus Wiener.

Dupuy, Alex. 2005. "From Jean-Bertrand Aristide to Gerard Latortue: The Unending Crisis of Democratization in Haiti". *Journal of Latin American Anthropology* 10 (1): 186–205.

Dupuy, Alex. 2007. *The Prophet and Power: Jean-Bertrand Aristide, the International Community, and Haiti.* Plymouth: Rowman & Littlefield.

Elwert, Georg. 1999. "Markets of Violence". In *Dynamics of Violence: Processes of Escalation and De-Escalation in Violent Group Conflicts*, edited by Georg Elwert et al., 85–102. Berlin: Duncker & Humblot.

Elwert, Georg. 2003. "Intervention in Markets of Violence". In *Potentials of Disorder: Explaining Conflict and Stability in the Caucasus and in the Former Yugoslavia*, edited by Jan Koehler and Christoph Zürcher, 219–243. Manchester: Manchester University Press.

Erickson, Amy. 2014. *Exploiting Inequalities: Conflict and Power Relations in Bel Air.* Oslo: Norwegian Church Aid.

Fatton Jr., Robert. 2002. *Haiti's Predatory Republic: The Unending Transition to Democracy.* Boulder: Lynne Rienner.

Fatton Jr., Robert. 2006. "Haiti: The Saturnalia of Emancipation and the Vicissitudes of Predatory Rule". *Third World Quarterly* 27 (1): 115–133.

Fatton Jr., Robert. 2007. *The Roots of Haitian Despotism.* Boulder: Lynne Rienner.

Fleurimond, Wiener Kerns. 2009. *Haïti de la Crise à l'Occupation, Histoire d'un Chaos (2000–2004) – Tome I: La Chute d'Aristide.* Paris: L'Harmattan.

Gambetta, Diego. 1996. *The Sicilian Mafia: The Business of Private Protection.* Cambridge: Harvard University Press.

Gros, Jean-Germain. 2012. *State Failure, Underdevelopment, and Foreign Intervention in Haiti.* London and New York: Routledge.

Hallward, Peter. 2007. *Damming the Flood: Haiti, Aristide and the Politics of Containment.* London and New York: Verso.

Hammond, Guy. 2012. *Saving Port-au-Prince: UN Efforts to Protect Civilians in Haiti in 2006–2007*. Washington, DC: The Stimson Center.

Herman, Eduardo Aldunate. 2010. *Backpacks Full of Hope: The UN Mission in Haiti*. Waterloo: Centre for International Governance Innovation and Wilfrid Laurier University Press.

International Crisis Group. 2006. *Haiti: Security and the Reintegration of the State*. Brussels: International Crisis Group.

Jean, Jean-Claude, and Marc Maesschalck. 1999. *Transition Politique en Haïti: Radiographie du Pouvoir Lavalas*. Paris: L'Harmattan.

Kemp, Walter, Mark Shaw, and Arthur Boutellis. 2013. *The Elephant in the Room: How Can Peace Operations Deal with Organized Crime?* New York: International Peace Institute.

Kivland, Chelsey Louise. 2009. *A Report on the Recent Changes in Perceptions of Security and Social Services in Bel Air, Haiti*. Geneva: Small Arms Survey.

Kivland, Chelsey Louise. 2014. "Becoming a Force in the Zone: Hedonopolitics, Masculinity, and the Quest for Respect on Haiti's Streets". *Cultural Anthropology* 29 (4): 672–698.

Kolbe, Athena. 2013. *Revisiting Haiti's Gangs and Organized Violence*. Rio de Janeiro: HASOW.

Kovats-Bernat, J. Christopher. 2006. *Sleeping Rough in Port-Au-Prince: An Ethnography of Street Children and Violence in Haiti*. Gainesville: University Press of Florida.

Lambach, Daniel. 2007. *Oligopolies of Violence in Post-Conflict Societies*. Hamburg: German Institute of Global and Area Studies.

Lunde, Henriette. 2012. *The Violent Lifeworlds of Young Haitians: Gangs as Livelihood in a Port-au-Prince Ghetto*. Oslo: Fafo.

Marcelin, Louis Herns. 2015. "Violence, Human Insecurity, and the Challenge of Rebuilding Haiti: A Study of a Shantytown in Port-au-Prince". *Current Anthropology* 56 (2): 230–255.

Mehler, Andreas. 2004. "Oligopolies of Violence in Africa South of the Sahara". *Nord-Süd-Aktuell* 18 (3): 539–548.

Mobekk, Eirin. 2008. "MINUSTAH and the Need for a Context-Specific Strategy: The Case of Haiti". In *Security Sector Reform and UN Integrated Missions: Experience From Burundi, the Democratic Republic of Congo, Haiti and Kosovo*, edited by Heiner Hänggi and Vincenza Scherrer, 113–168. Münster: Lit Verlag.

Mobekk, Eirin, and Anne M. Street. 2006. *Disarmament, Demobilisation and Reintegration: What Role should the EU Play in Haiti? Recommendations for Change*. London: ActionAid.

Muggah, Robert. 2013. "The Political Economy of Statebuilding in Haiti: Informal Resistance to Security-first Statebuilding". In *Political Economy of Statebuilding: Power After Peace*, edited by Mats Berdal and Dominik Zaum, 293–305. London and New York: Routledge.

Neiburg, Federico, Natacha Nicaise, and Pedro Braum. 2011. *Leaders in Bel Air*. Rio de Janeiro: Viva Rio.

Nicolas, Mireille. 2006. *Haïti, d'un Coup d'État à l'Autre*. Paris: L'Harmattan.

Peirce, Jennifer. 2007. "Protection for Whom? Stabilization and Coercive Rule in Haiti". *Paterson Review of International Affairs* 8: 96–112.

Perito, Robert M., and Michael Dziedzic. 2008. *Haiti: Confronting the Gangs of Port-au-Prince*. Washington, DC: United States Institute of Peace.

RNDDH. 2012. *Affaire Brandt: Le RNDDH Exige l'Aboutissement de l'Enquête Ouverte et le Jugement de Tous les Membres du Gang*. Port-au-Prince: Réseau National de Défense des Droits Humains.

Rodgers, Dennis. 2007. "Gangs, Violence and Asset Building". In *Reducing Global Poverty: The Case for Asset Accumulation*, edited by Caroline O. N. Moser, 179–195. Washington, DC: Brookings Institution Press.

Schuberth, Moritz. 2014. "The Impact of Drug Trafficking on Informal Security Actors in Kenya". *Africa Spectrum* 49 (3): 55–81.

Schuberth, Moritz. 2015a. "The Challenge of Community-based Armed Groups: Towards a Conceptualization of Militias, Gangs, and Vigilantes". *Contemporary Security Policy* 36 (2): 296–320.

Schuberth, Moritz. 2015b. "A Transformation from Political to Criminal Violence? Politics, Organised Crime and the Shifting Functions of Haiti's Urban Armed Groups". *Conflict, Security & Development* 15 (2): 169–196.

Schuberth, Moritz. 2016a. "Beyond Gang Truces and *Mano Dura* Policies: Towards Substitutive Security Governance in Latin America". *Stability: International Journal of Security & Development* 5 (1): Art. 17.

Schuberth, Moritz. 2016b. "Growing the Grassroots or Backing Bandits? Dilemmas of Donor Support for Haiti's (Un)Civil Society". *Journal of Peacebuilding & Development* 11 (1): 93–98.

Schuberth, Moritz. 2017a. "Disarmament, Demobilisation and Reintegration in Unconventional Settings: The Case of MINUSTAH's Community Violence Reduction". *International Peacekeeping* 24 (3): 410–433.

Schuberth, Moritz. 2017b. "To Engage or Not to Engage Haiti's Urban Armed Groups? Safe Access in Disaster-stricken and Conflict-affected Cities". *Environment and Urbanization* 29 (2): 425–442.

Schuberth, Moritz. 2018a. "Divergent Worldviews among Peacebuilders: Evidence From Haiti". In *Blame, Sway, and Vigilante Tactics: How Other Cultures Think Differently and Implications for Planning*, edited by Gwyneth Sutherlin, 9–16. Washington, DC: US Department of Defense.

Schuberth, Moritz. 2018b. "Hybrid Security Governance, Post-election Violence and the Legitimacy of Community-based Armed Groups in Urban Kenya". *Journal of Eastern African Studies* 12 (2): 386–404.

Sprague, Jeb. 2012. *Paramilitarism and the Assault on Democracy in Haiti*. New York: Monthly Review Press.

Tilly, Charles. 1985. "War Making and State Making as Organized Crime". In *Bringing the State Back In*, edited by Peter Evans et al., 169–187. Cambridge: Cambridge University Press.

Volkov, Vadim. 2002. *Violent Entrepreneurs: The Use of Force in the Making of Russian Capitalism*. Ithaca and London: Cornell University Press.

Wilentz, Amy. 1989. *The Rainy Season: Haiti since Duvalier*. New York: Simon and Schuster.

Willman, Alys, and Louis Herns Marcelin. 2010. "'If They Could Make Us Disappear, They Would'! Youth and Violence in Cite Soleil, Haiti". *Journal of Community Psychology* 38 (4): 515–531.

3 Security blurs and citizenship
Consequences in Indonesia

Laurens Bakker

Introduction

March 20, 2018, I am walking at night along Cikini Raya street in Central Jakarta. Here one easily sees the dynamics of life in this urban zone. As a stream of cars and motorcycles passes by, passengers alight from buses and (motor)taxis to enter the street's shops, clinics, offices and restaurants. Others eat at the many street vendor stalls or wait between the carts and chairs for their chance to cross or to hail transportation. The place is packed, but few signs of security concerns or security provision are visible. A single sign posted on the side warns passers-by to be vigilant against pickpockets. A few police officers man a small post below the train station. Occasionally, traffic police on motors with blaring sirens clear a route through the traffic for a high-ranking government official's car. Sitting down at a roadside eatery provides me with a more nuanced view of the surroundings. Many of the permanent restaurants and shops, even the simple, wooden shack-like structures, have private CCTV cameras. The flag of *Pemuda Pancasila*, a national *ormas* or vigilante group, hangs from a shop's sidewall.[1] A few young men appear to loiter at a fence, but are keeping a steady eye on what is going on. Private security guards sit near the entries of the major offices set back from the street. Another customer at the eatery, a local resident living just behind Cikini Raya, tells me how his neighbours came across a thief a few weeks ago and beat him up thoroughly before handing him over to the police. They put the neighbourhood watch on extra alert. "The situation has deteriorated", he tells me,

> A few years ago FPI would often carry out sweepings and demonstrations along the street, which also kept criminals out. Now we only get occasional HMI demonstrations and those youngsters only bring unrest. Criminals are not afraid here now, they shoot the police![2]

The eatery's cook disagreed, as he felt that for him little had changed. He got his immediate protection from a group of local tough guys, known by such diverse names as *preman, jago* or *jawara*, whom he paid a weekly fee. They helped with troublesome customers and kept thieves and other criminals away. If he did not pay them, they would beat him up or burn his stall, he was quite certain, but he had no intention of resisting. Their protection was quite good and their fee affordable. Besides, they had a strong reputation for martial art skills. They also were on friendly terms with the police at the train station post, so the vendor did not think he had much of an alternative.

The existence of multiple and diverse providers of security, some of whom pose security threats themselves, is not unique for Cikini Raya. Throughout Indonesia this diversity of providers gives rise to a "security blur" in which civilian and state policing actors co-exist in dynamic relations of collaboration and competition while dealing with the (in)security of the population. Two critical dimensions largely define the range and tolerance of their activities: dedication to the general good, as expressed in performance, appearance and discourse and effectiveness. While the latter simply refers to capabilities demonstrated by getting things done, the former is of a more complex nature since the general good might refer both to the nation as a whole – whose interests may be damaged by secessionist movements, or criminal activities – and to the specific population group such security actors seek to represent. Balancing these two is important: insufficient emphasis on national unity or too many disruptive activities may give state authorities reason to crack down on non-state security providers, while neglecting the populations' actual security needs can cause providers to lose support and become marginalised. Yet securing the nation sits uneasily with the agendas of non-state security groups that embed specific foci in terms of religion or ethnicity in their approach to security; emphases which imply a stratified citizenship rather than national unity. As I will argue in what follows, such citizenship is a spectre that should not be ignored.

In this chapter I seek to analyse the implications of such blurred security provision for the quality of citizenship. By discussing a variety of "security blurs" that appear in terms of actors, (in)formalities and ensuing actions, I approach security as part of the "complex bundle of practices constituting political membership" (Lazar 2013, 12) that jointly form citizenship. My central point of concern is that while *ormas* provide security to and strengthen the citizenship of some, they are a source of insecurity to others. Does the existence of multiple security providers indicate a stratified citizenship, or do these security blurs strengthen mutual cohesion in society?

Vigilantism and citizenship

Vigilantism and citizenship are strongly related to each other in that both concern membership and political representation. Vigilantism is a worldwide phenomenon of localised, self-policing groups, often with links to crime and roots in local culture, that seek to maintain a specific notion of order and security in (part of) society (after Sen and Pratten 2007, 1). Vigilantes frequently explain their actions and the reason for their existence in terms of lacunae in the provision of justice, security and governance caused by incompetent, undemocratic or corrupt state officials (e.g. Goldstein 2003; Sen and Pratten 2007; Sundar 2010; Petrus 2015; Wilson and Bakker 2016). If part of the population is thus reduced to lower class citizens by means of captured state functions, this can be a direct reason for popular support of vigilantism in defence of citizenship status (Oomen 2004; Telle 2013; Van Stapele 2016). In these terms, vigilantism can be seen as a reaction to a citizenship of scales in which the relations between state and non-state, elites and non-elites are negotiated (cf. Werbner 2004) in which the local political community, rather than the nation state is the focus of identification (Lazar 2013, 12). Stokke (2017, 24) argues that citizenship is made up of four key dimensions; membership, legal status, rights and participation, which come together in dynamic constellations in which the form and substance of different groups' citizenship are defined by competing interests, strategies and capacities in diverse political arenas.

Ormas locate themselves at the interface between vigilantism and citizenship. They present themselves using a discourse that emphasises unity, equality, social justice and democracy as key values, but which is hampered by a membership that is based on identity – regional, ethnic, religious – rather than on a shared sense of nationality (see Bertrand 2004; Van Klinken 2007). While real provision of security to many can go a long way in downplaying such emphasis on identity, such a base may also provide a platform for the establishment of powerful patron-client relations, which have a strong role in state-making in Indonesian society age. Ford and Pepinsky (2014) and Berenschot et al. (2017, 10–17) point out how local, physically present leaders and organisations are preferred over the abstract, anonymous institutions of the national state, which remains strongly associated with notions of corruption and nepotism. As such, local security providers are important factors in community building (Bubandt 2005). On the level of the street and the neighbourhood, their activities are strongly interwoven with notions of who is part of the local community and who is not. Vigilance against "outsiders" is historically encouraged as government policy, but is also a cause for swift and united action by local actors in dealing – at times cruelly – with outside intruders, as exemplified by the neighbours beating up a thief in Cikini Raya (see also Colombijn 2002; Bakker 2017a).

This raises the question of how the provision of security impacts the lives of individual citizens. In-, and exclusion of individuals in local society as per the *ormas'* definition make the notion of citizenship important in the practice of security provision, particularly given the frequency – as we will see below here – with which security providers refer to their societal licence to act as they do. A local-level provision of security that appears beyond the control of official authorities and that differentiates between citizens along religious or ethnic lines can cause inequality and tensions as much as the abuse of government powers against which *ormas* agitate. Often, local communities overcome such tensions through critical scrutinisation of local security actors' actions (cf. Bakker 2017b; Wilson 2017). This makes that while *ormas* constitute a visible part in the provision and maintenance of day-to-day (in)security, their roots in the local community make them dependent on popular support and vulnerable to public disapproval.

Events on Cikini Raya illustrate that what is sketched in the above can be studied as a variety of security blurs in which emphasis could be placed on the security actors, their authority, the trust vested in them and the in- and exclusion they propagate. Although tension and uncertainty feature minimally in the vignette above, demonstrations by FPI worry restaurant owners selling alcohol, café and karaoke parlour visitors, as well as artists meeting and exhibiting at the Taman Ismail Marzuki art centre that sits prominently on the street. FPI's stern religious outlook does not hold with such businesses and expressions. The Pemuda Pancasila flag indicates however that this group, rather than FPI is controlling the area, and "PP" is more lenient in religious issues as long as locals pay membership or security fees. PP has less influence with HMI than FPI does, however, and has for some years been engaged in turf wars with FBR, an ethnic Betawi *ormas*. Each of these groups is favoured by different parts of the population: FPI emphasises Islamic values, FBR Betawi interests while PP supports a conductive business climate and disposes of links to powerful patrons. Local people hence join all these *ormas* and may hold membership of more than one. Depending on local events, threats and necessities one or the other gains most support. As such, *ormas* are a manifestation of the importance of the local level of citizenship vis-à-vis that of the state, but also demonstrate how their emphasis on specific identity traits might mark some as lower-levels citizens in a way that the state does not recognise.

Informal security providers

State functionaries, youth groups, ethnic and religious organisations, gangsters and street thugs who complement and overlap each other, but also compete for influence and territory, carry out Indonesia's security provision. Schulte Nordholt (1991), in a historical study, writes how in (pre) colonial times, each area would have its *jago*: literally a "fighting cock", but meaning a "daredevil" or a "strongman" when in reference to a person. The *jago* would act as go-between for the rulers and local communities. He would maintain order and, for instance, collect taxes on the ruler's behalf. At the same time he would, for a fee, turn a blind eye to illegal activities by the local population and speak for them if taxes were too hefty. The *jago* would also engage in crime. Generally versed in martial arts, armed, able to summon henchmen to his assistance and made invulnerable through magic protection (*kekebalan*), he could levy private local taxes and steal from the population with relative impunity. He thus balanced fear and protection. Fear, instilled by his own physical prowess and his demonstrated willingness to use violence. Protection, as he would keep criminals and snooping government authorities out of "his" area. As such, a *jago* was no Hobsbaw-mian "noble bandit", but rather a ruthless entrepreneur who occupied a powerful position between society and its rulers. By strategically controlling the flow of information, goods and labour between the two, he ensured himself of profit and control.

In more recent times, the position, function and activities in the provision of security embodied in the *jago* are associated with *preman* organised in *ormas*. Like the *jago*, a *preman* connotes criminality, a "devil-may-care" attitude, as well as a measure of social responsibility to those part of the *preman*'s ethnic or religious group. In colloquial Indonesian, *preman* connotes "street thug" or "hoodlum".[3] They are usually young, male and hang out on the street where they run protection rackets among street vendors and market sellers, provide security to brothels and prostitutes, sell drugs on the streets, manage street-corner gambling operations and are not beyond theft, burglary or the occasional robbery. As such, they regularly run afoul of the police whom they know well as authorities to watch out for, but also as competitors and employers (see below). *Preman* are willing to take on the police in street brawls if the stakes are high enough which ensures them of social popularity as few dare to discipline the police. Moving into the lacunae left open by a poorly functioning legal system, *preman* provide security to those who otherwise forego it and collect debts that would otherwise remain unpaid. Crime is part of their means of earning revenue, but so are representing the underclass to the authorities and servicing its needs (cf. Heriyanto 2013; Wiwoho 2017). As with the *jago*, the vignette *preman* connotes a sense of cockiness, of pride. A strong, leading *preman* is often known as the *jago* of his group and as an important figure in local society. For today's *preman*, the display of one's dedication to the needs of the population are important elements of one's societal credibility. Publicly criticising and resisting government, showing no fear and using violence are part of this attitude (Wilson 2012; Bakker 2017b). As an *ormas* leader in Balikpapan, the business capital of the province of East Kalimantan, explained this attitude to me:

> Of course we use violence, we have to. Otherwise people do not believe in us, but we do it in an exact and precise way so people know and understand. Never just beat somebody up, that confuses people! Recently we beat up this corrupt cop who was making a nuisance of himself demanding way too many bribes from shopkeepers (laughs). We did it in the dark, but all the shopkeepers know it was us and why it happened.
>
> (Interview, December 2017)

I asked whether he was not worried that he would be arrested for this, given that if the shopkeepers know, it is likely that the police know as well:

> Sure they know, but they are not going to arrest us! Let them prove it, innocent until proven is the law in Indonesia! Besides, the chief of police

does not like corruption at all. I am sure he supports the punishment [of the officer]. He would be quite embarrassed if this case became public.
(Interview, December 2017)

Such an outspoken attitude and what is more, a physical punitive correction of the functioning of the police, is in line with how many *ormas* and *preman* present themselves: as looking after the wellbeing of "their" citizens and dealing with such threats as outsiders – police or not – may pose. Such brazenness can be a conscious strategy to confront a threat or force a decision. Examples include, for instance, a *preman* leader who in 2013 drove his motorbike into the Depok district court of law and proceeded to destroy the interior in order to pressure the chairing judge to pass judgement in favour of him and the people he represented (see Bakker 2017b, 140–142). On the majority-Muslim island of Lombok *preman* enacted public sentiments by preventing the inauguration of a Hindu temple (Telle 2013, 206), while FBR and *Pemuda Pancasila* regularly clash in public mass fights for control over profitable areas of Jakarta (Pramono 2015). Usually such actions end in the arrests of (some of) the *preman*. In part this is the point: it shows that one has the courage to act and face the consequences, but an arrest also serves to demonstrate how long it takes one to be released. The sooner, the better one's *beking* (backing) through patronage. As such, the acts that *preman* and *ormas* undertake in the name of ensuring local security and defending local interests frequently constitute a blurring of criminality and social concern. "Who polices the police?" a *preman* night-watchman asked me in Jakarta in 2016. "We do", he answered his own question. "Others are afraid or corrupt, especially the police themselves. Only we dare to act if necessary, so we do [it]". When I asked him who then polices the *ormas* he told me that this was done through societal (dis)approval. If the local people felt that their security providers had gone too far, they would no longer allow them to operate within their community. I expressed my doubt, having seen local *preman* intimidating locals for kickbacks and "gifts". Grinning, he answered that this happened indeed, but only to immigrants new to the area who could not be considered locals and that anyway, the local, powerful "bosses" did not object and would protect them in case of complaints. Membership of local society thus appeared to exist in degrees of inclusion and vulnerability. "Real locals" and immigrants without a sufficiently strong local network hold different statuses, while local patronage provides *preman* with a degree of immunity against societal displeasure.

Non-state security groups in a nationalist perspective

Most *ormas* leaders I spoke with placed the origin of *premanisme* in the early 1970s, around the time President Suharto came to power. These were tumultuous times culminating in the killing of between half a million and three million people as communists by the army, police and irregular groups of gangsters and religious militias. Such irregular armed groups featured

56 Laurens Bakker

prominently in Indonesian nationalist history: criminal gangs in Jakarta had formed guerrilla units fighting against the returning Dutch after the second World War (Cribb 1991), while throughout the archipelago armed groups were fighting for independence before there was a national Indonesian army.

Following Indonesia's independence some of these groups dissolved themselves while others merged into the national army, yet throughout the nation groups set themselves up as local strongmen. Connections between these, the army, police, local government officials and entrepreneurs allowed for the development of patrimonial relationships in which the strongmen received protection against the law from their patrons in exchange for a share in the profits and the service of their muscles. Thus, informal violence became institutionalised as a means for the representatives of the state to intimidate and extort, and to finance the crony capitalism for which Suharto's New Order regime would become famous. This blending of crime and authority led some observers to conclude that the regime operated like a criminal gang, governing as a *"preman* state" (Lindsey 2001) in which violence and extortion were normalised as state practice. Simultaneously, the regime argued that far-reaching securitisation of the nation was absolutely necessary to protect the young state against multiple threats. Official communications emphasised the need to remain vigilant against internal enemies (such as communists) as well as expansionist foreign powers (Siegel 1998). Among the population a "trained citizenry" (*rakyat terlatih*) was developed who could assist the military in national defence through a variety of civil defence groups ("*hansip*", *pertahanan sipil*). However, these groups lacked the reputation of the *preman* who by and large declined to join these new, regime-controlled groups given their established influence and *beking*.

Preman organised in groups affiliated to key persons in the army, police or elite. These carried out the regime's dirty work through these patrons, such as controlling labourers on strike, clearing settled land for redevelopment, repressing opposition and student movements and maintaining links to organised crime. Yet numerous "wild *preman*" remained over whom the regime lacked control. In the spring of 1983, the regime began to subject these by killing them in a campaign that lasted roughly two years and saw between 5,000 and 10,000 people killed as *preman*. Their corpses were frequently mutilated and left where they would be found and viewed by a large public (Barker 1998). The result was that *preman* in general became subservient to the regime and authorities, to the extent that "if *preman* were seen to carry out criminal acts in public there was no point in reporting to the police, as these had probably sent the *preman* to begin with".[4] The regime thus consciously blurred security provision: *preman* were intimidated into an association with officialdom in order to do its dirty work and criminal business, yet were so also secured from the lethal violence of the police. Simultaneously, the regime urged its citizens to be vigilant against (abstract) threats to the nation and its unity while also exposing them to crime and injustice carried out by *preman* on its behalf. For citizens the regime ensured and enacted day-to-day security through its official functions and actions, yet it could also threaten them with impunity through their *preman* fellow citizens if that was economically or politically profitable. The security provided hence emphasised the needs and interests of the regime over those of the citizens.

In 1998 a combination of prolonged economic crisis and wide public dissatisfaction over the regime's authoritarian rule and conspicuous self-enrichment led to its downfall. As riots and, in some areas, major bloody conflicts erupted across the archipelago, many observers were startled and at a loss to explain such violence.[5] "*Disintegrasi*" of the nation became a recurring theme in the news as analysts pointed out the army's and police's apparent inability to quell the violence and the distinctly local natures of the conflicts taking place. In 1998, President Habibie promulgated new national legislation that severed the tight reins of New Order governance by decentralising considerable administrative and fiscal authority to lower levels of government. Combined with a major increase in the democratic quality of society by allowing for new political parties, freer press and an active civil society, these measures ensured a much larger role for the lower levels of the administration in governing Indonesia. This allowed for greater emphasis on local interests, which spurred the rise of new actors and the coming into existence of locally focused new security blurs in which local actors took a critical stance towards government and regime-representation as a rallying point for popular representation. A proliferation of *ormas* as *preman*-like organisations under the denominator of democratisation and citizens' rights was not what observers of Indonesia's booming democratisation had expected, yet this is what happened.

Ormas and local security

The decentralisation of administrative and fiscal authority empowered the governmental levels of the provinces (*propinsi*) and the lower district (*kabupaten*) and municipality (*kota*) levels in economic development and taxation policies. Regional economies became important arenas and civil organisations began to emerge that propagated the interests of specific ethnic groups. Often these concerned indigenous groups asking for recognition of customary rights to land and resources, but also organisations of sizeable minorities. These organisations frequently registered as *ormas* to ensure legality and visibility.

Effectively these organisations gave two types of arguments to legitimise their existence. First is the need to guard and protect local society and the unity of the Republic of Indonesia by furthering social justice and prosperity, peaceful co-existence among the local population and countering of anti-nationalist and radical thoughts and expressions. Tasks in which the *ormas* supplement the police and the army, but also provide unique qualities through its members' profound knowledge of local society. Second is the need for greater representation of the interests and culture of the (ethnic) group within the local society in which the *ormas* exists. The overall argument sustaining all actions is the provision of security, either aimed at a local situation or based on arguments of national importance. Yet the constituting argument is one of popular trust and knowledge, which the police lacks at this high level. As the aforementioned *ormas* leader in Balikpapan put it:

> We help the people, and we help the authorities. Often police or soldiers have less understanding of what goes on locally than we do. After all, we live here, we are locals, we know the people and the culture. Police and soldiers live separated from society and hence lack insight. We help them in understanding. People often ask us to help, rather than go to the police. Why? Because they know us. We are neighbours, family . . . the police are migrants, they come from other parts of Indonesia.
>
> (Interview, June 2016)

In doing so, *ormas* require recognition and visibility to have their claims validated. Recognition depends largely on dependability and success. If *ormas* manage to obtain results for the people they strive to represent – such as access to land, jobs and indemnifications – their reputation increases, particularly if the results effectively trickle down to the population. If they fail to secure such results or if it is clear that they are simply muscle for hire to the highest bidder, their support tends to decrease. Recognition and support also depend on the capacity and willingness of the *ormas* to use violence in securing the interests of their constituency. As with the *preman* discussed earlier, *ormas* need to prove that they stand for their actions and are willing to risk conflict to get their results. Contrary to "traditional" *preman* activity, however, *ormas* frequently make a point of justifying their actions in terms of official legality whenever possible. The chair of the legal aid department of an ethnic Dayak *ormas* in Samarinda, the capital of the province of East Kalimantan, gave the following example:

> You see, if a farmer's customary land is taken from him unlawfully by a plantation or another company, we help him bring the case to the court. He cannot do that alone, he does not know the law. It will be very difficult to win, but the law prescribes that he must receive a reasonable indemnification. We tell the judge that we will read the decision carefully, and that we will not object to the decision if it is reached and explained in accordance with the law. If it is not, we step back and the security wing comes to visit. The judge may then explain the decision to them.
>
> (Interview, June 2016)

The security wing mentioned here is a highly visibility element of the *ormas*. These are fit men dressed in camouflage uniforms, ethnic jewellery, sunglasses and combat boots who parade along the street and stand to attention during official events. They only wear such uniforms when an official presence of the security wing is required, such as at meetings, parades and so on. If security is to be enforced or other violence is to take place, this is done by massed members without tags or uniforms that might make them easy to identify. The legality of *ormas* violence remains a problematic issue and while police and army tend to condone it if it serves to calm matters down, fighting in official uniform is often considered as challenging the authorities and as such a disproportionate risk. In most *ormas* the security wings are highly influential elements. They often have a substantial number of *preman* among their personnel. While these may join for the security and legitimacy that the *ormas* provides, many of those I spoke to appeared genuinely enthusiastic about their *ormas'* purposes and were hopeful of its success.

Many of today's *ormas* have been (co-)founded by *jago*, sensitive to the changing times and aware that civil society and societal support today may offer better patronage than relations with local power holders do. The organisations' image hence is often carefully managed, and considerable attention is given to providing proof of social responsibility and activities aimed at the greater good of society. Importantly, in recent years several *ormas* have greatly added to their reputation by being first on the scene in case of natural disasters and providing faster and more organised assistance than government or the military.[6] *Ormas* generally dispose of an excellent organisational structure that follows military lines and distinguishes commanders, sub-commanders, squads as well as a "civilian" apparatus. The larger *ormas* dispose of guard posts within their territories where people can reach them in case of unrest. Through mobile phones, WhatsApp and BlackBerry Messenger, members can be mobilised very quickly. For instance, while I was visiting a local guard post in Jakarta in January 2015, a neighbour came running in reporting the theft of a motorcycle by a group of unknown youngsters. The guard immediately got on his phone and within minutes, a group of some twenty members on ten to fifteen motorcycles and armed with clubs and machetes assembled in front of the post and set off to give chase. When I asked the guard whether he would call the police as well, he answered that this was up to the man who reported the theft, but that personally he would not bother as the police were always slow to arrive, even slower in catching somebody and then would let him go in exchange for a bribe. If his group would not catch the thief, they would alert the posts in other neighbourhoods and see whether the stolen motor would surface there. They had the plate number, so he thought they stood a good chance.

Such an aggressive and swift reaction is largely possible because the *ormas* included the street *preman* from the area in their membership. While the *ormas* considered this a control of crime – the members were to follow the *ormas'* rules – it also meant that they gained control over elements of crime in society, such as protection racketeering, informal parking businesses and purportedly the local small-scale gambling operations. One of their leaders explained to me that society condoned this. The *ormas* members had to make a living, and a certain degree of informal and criminal activities did not raise eyebrows. Rather, it showed the *ormas'* prowess in that they could control these environments as well. The point was, he felt, to know what society would tolerate and when the *ormas' preman* might go too far. Should that happen, or if they were arrested by the police for proven crimes, the *ormas* would not back them up.

As such, the security blurs in which *preman* and official security actors jointly operate have altered in comparison to those of the New order era. Rather than as protégées and extensions of the power of the regime or its local representatives, *ormas* today argue to act on behalf of the population and emphasise civil duties and democracy in their reasons for acting as they do. As such, the "boss" has become much more diffuse and *ormas'* agency increased markedly. Local interests take pride of place, but who and what constitutes the local for these *ormas* is frequently defined and mobilised along ethnic or religious lines. The quality of local citizenship thus includes elements that are not available to all, but that are maintained by these informal security providers.

Relations with formal security providers

In the above, the police come to the fore mostly as ineffective at best and troublesome at worst. Nevertheless, both the police and the military are present throughout Indonesian society and informal security providers do have to contend with their activities and influence. While *ormas* can be said to have gained popular legitimacy by taking up civil society functions, the police continue to suffer from a poor reputation among many Indonesian citizens. In part, these perceptions may be caused by the fact that most Indonesians only come in contact with traffic police, a part of the police force notorious for demanding bribes (cf. Davies et al. 2016). Another reason might be the police's perceived lenient treatment of criminals, who are thought to be let go if they pay the arresting officers a sufficient bribe (Colombijn 2002).[7] Such notions of the police portray them as corrupt and inefficient. In part, the bribery image is not without ground. During a series of discussions with traffic police and other officers in East Kalimantan in 2010, they explained to me that they had to pay a hefty bribe to be selected for a local police force. To do so, they needed to borrow money. Once they were on the force they were expected to repay within a reasonable period, usually some two years, given that they now had a prestigious job. At the same time, however, others would come asking for financial support, which, as a person with a position of standing, the newly sworn-in officer could not refuse without damaging their newly acquired status. Furthermore, their direct chef expected percentages of bribes collected by his staff to come his way. Without these it was difficult to curry favour or earn a promotion. For street officers, relations with local *preman* hence are conductive to their own needs. As *preman* pay officers part of the income of their protection rackets and other activities, the officers turn a blind eye. The *preman* come out and support the officers when the police call upon civilian assistance in clean-up actions and other more symbolic operations, and the officers warn the *preman* ahead of planned actions that might threaten their illegal sources of income (see Tadié and Permanadeli 2015).

While such a collaboration at the street level benefits both officers and *preman*, it is higher up, at the level of the district head of police and the leadership of *ormas*, that political ties become more prominent and beneficial. While travelling in a protected forest zone in East Kalimantan in summer 2016, my local colleague and myself noticed illegal logging operations taking place. When we hailed the loggers – who turned out to be members of a *preman* group from a nearby area – they told us that their boss was the local police sub-district police commander. Seeing our incredulous faces, they told us to look for their trucks at the police station as that is where they parked in the evening and to note the log pile behind the station. While the sub-district commander was not available to see us, log buyers confirmed his role to me. Baker (2015), writing on Indonesia's off-budget economy and national police, shows that it is at this level that police chiefs are capable of amassing considerable wealth. These regional police heads are, according to Baker (2015), part of networks of state, non-state and grey area brokers that have come to the fore in the dynamic climate of administrative decentralisation. In the regions these include heads of police, military, government, the judiciary, entrepreneurs and *ormas* leaders, who can facilitate as well as waylay police projects. As such, it is generally beneficial for *ormas* and police to collaborate and allow one another space to move. It is not uncommon for heads of police at this level to be honorary members of local *ormas*, or at least grace their official gatherings with their presence. This does not mean that the two collaborate continuously: *ormas* will demonstrate against police actions if their interests or those of the people they represent require this. Likewise, *ormas* will carry out mass actions and threaten unrest against third parties even if this embarrasses police authority. Examples of such are indigenous peoples *ormas* in Kalimantan closing roads to plantation firms, or holding demonstrations in government centres that may turn violent if they are not met by officials to discuss their grievances.

Relations between *ormas* and the military are generally good. While the army generally is in charge of the most valuable security projects, such as guarding oil companies and mining operations, they will employ local *ormas* in subordinate functions. Also, in reference to the "trained citizenry" (*rakyat terlatih*) principle as defenders of Indonesia's territory and unity, the Ministry of Defence in 2015 introduced the *Bela Negara* (Defend the State) programme. *Bela Negara* aims to provide military training to a force of 100,000 reservists throughout the country, with *ormas* members being prime recipients of these trainings. A relevant example of resulting collaboration is that between Brigade Manguni, an *ormas* based in North Sulawesi, close to the island of Mindanao in the Philippines, and the Ministry of Defence.

Brigade Manguni has been given tasks in patrolling the communities in the area and keeping an eye out for strangers, especially non-Indonesians, in an effort to prevent terrorists from entering Indonesia from Mindanao. As locals with a wide-ranging network of connections and members, Brigade Manguni is more knowledgeable and better informed of arrivals of foreigners then both the military and the police.

Concluding remarks

The provision of security in Indonesia is the domain of multiple actors: police officers, street *preman, ormas*, the military and others, who interact in ways that are sustained by legal as well as illegal elements, popular and populist sentiment, and an underlying continuous appeal to nationalist interests. The resulting "security blurs" are dynamic: they are shaped and influenced by the specific contexts of the localities where they take place, which may be cultural, religious, ethnic, economic and so on, and which define what is at stake as well as how power relations can be brought to bear effect. In-, and exclusion of individuals in the resulting security arrangements has important consequences as it defines their vulnerability to the predatory elements that security providers guard against as well as pose. All security providers, state as well as non-state, straddle the line between legality and illegality in their actions, thus continuing an established interlinkage that is tolerated by the majority group as long as the impact for them is not too severe. The measure of one's membership of local society and the ability to exert influence in its security issues thus are elementary factors in the quality of one's citizenship: the examples of the cook at the Jalan Cikini Raya eatery and the illegally logging police sub-district commander in East Kalimantan illustrate just how relevant one's position in this is in terms of power and control. Non-state security providers like *ormas*, as well as officials like the police, are protectors to the majority, criminals to some and employees to others. Such differences in position indicate the relevance of security providers' capacities to set conditions in terms of indigeneity, ethnicity, religion and locality. These are elements which impact upon the quality of citizenship of those affected. If such elements are enforced, the danger of an informal stratified citizenship is far from unrealistic. What seem to prevent this from happening to any great extent are the dynamism and the negotiated nature of the collaborations in which security provision is taking place, as caused by the differing agendas and constituencies of the diverse providers.

Notes

1 "*Ormas*" stands for *organisasi kemasyarakatan*, or societal organisation. This is a broad legal category that includes all sorts of organisations with a stated societal purpose such as sport organisations, aid foundations and health providers. Greenpeace and the World Wildlife Fund, for instance, also qualify as *ormas*.

2 FPI, Front Pembela Islam (Islamic Defenders Front) is a well-known vigilante group. For some time they carried out demonstrations along Cikini Raya, calling for a more stringent observance of Islamic teachings in society and politics. They also carried out "sweepings" in which they confiscated alcohol and drugs from (illegal) street vendors. This stopped after the local government began to take a harsher stance towards such actions following inter-vigilante fighting elsewhere in Jakarta. HMI, Himpunan Mahasiswa Islam (Islamic Students Association) has a lesser reputation for violence, but has its Jakarta secretariat around the corner of Cikini Raya. The statement that criminals go around the area shooting police officials is exaggerated, but an officer had indeed been shot in the street in January 2018, a few weeks prior to the conversation (see Poskotanews.com 2018).

3 For a more detailed discussion of the role of *preman* and the origins of the term, see Ryter (1998) and Wilson (2006). The word *preman* is thought to originate from the Dutch "vrij man" (free man) or possibly vrijman, a colonial era agent who was not an employee of the VOC, but deferred to their jurisdiction and operated under their permit. As such, he was not beyond the grasp of authority, but not controlled by it either (Ryter 1998, 51).

4 As explained by a Jakartan NGO activist, December 2017.

5 See Van Klinken (2007, 15–52) for an overview of explanations.

6 Examples of such recent actions of which I am aware include the provision of food and drinking water to villages isolated by mudslides by Brigade Manguni in North Sulawesi in 2014 and 2017; FPI's recurring food and goods distribution and soup kitchens during Jakarta's annual flooding; Laskar Bali's assistance in the provision of aid during Bali's Gunung Agung 2017 eruption; and Banser's 2017 assistance to victims of floods and mudslides in Pacitan, East Java.

7 This notion causes citizens to punish apprehended criminal themselves to ensure their neighbourhood's reputation for security, rather than hand them over for arrest and trial (see Bakker 2017a).

References

Baker, Jacqui. 2015. "The Rhizome State: Democratizing Indonesia's Off-Budget Economy". *Critical Asian Studies* 47 (2): 309–336.

Bakker, Laurens. 2017a. "Lynching, Public Violence and the Internet in Indonesia". In *Global Lynching and Collective Violence. Volume 1 Asia, Africa and the Middle-East*, edited by Michael J. Pfeifer, 10–33. Urbana and Chicago: University of Illinois Press.

Bakker, Laurens. 2017b. "Militias, Security and Citizenship in Indonesia". In *Citizenship and Democratization in Southeast Asia*, edited by Ward Berenschot, Henk Schulte Nordholt, and Laurens Bakker, 125–154. Leiden and Boston: Brill.

Barker, Joshua. 1998. "State of Fear: Controlling the Criminal Contagion in Suharto's New Order". *Indonesia* 66 (October): 6–43.

Berenschot, Ward, Henk Schulte Nordholt, and Laurens Bakker. 2017. "Introduction: Citizenship and Democratization in Postcolonial Southeast Asia". In *Citizenship and Democratization in Southeast Asia*, edited by Ward Berenschot, Henk Schulte Nordholt, and Laurens Bakker, 1–30. Leiden and Boston: Brill.

Bertrand, Jacques. 2004. *Nationalism and Ethnic Conflict in Indonesia*. Cambridge: Cambridge University Press.

Bubandt, Nils. 2005. "Vernacular Security: The Politics of Feeling Safe in Global, National and Local Worlds". *Security Dialogue* 36 (3): 275–296.

Colombijn, Freek. 2002. "Maling, Maling! The Lynching of Petty Criminals". In *Roots of Violence in Indonesia*, edited by Freek Colombijn and Thomas Lindblad, 299–330. Leiden: KITLV Press.

Cribb, Robert. 1991. *Gangsters and Revolutionaries: The Jakarta People's Militia and the Indonesian Revolution 1945–1949*. Honolulu: University of Hawai'i Press.

Davies, Sharyn Graham, Adrianus Meliala, and John Buttle. 2016. "Gangnam Style Versus Eye of the Tiger: People, Police and Procedural Justice in Indonesia". *Policing and Society* 26 (4): 453–474.

Ford, Michelle, and Thomas B. Pepinsky, eds. 2014. *Beyond Oligarchy: Wealth, Power and Contemporary Indonesian Politics*. Ithaca: Cornell Southeast Asia Program Publications.

Goldstein, Daniel. 2003. "'In Our Own Hands': Lynching, Justice and the Law in Bolivia". *American Ethnologist* 30 (1): 22–43.

Heriyanto, Anni. 2013. "Berteman Dengan Preman". *Kompas*, April 3, 2013. https://olahraga.kompas.com/read/2013/04/03/04252037/berteman.dengan.preman.

Lazar, Sian. 2013. *The Anthropology of Citizenship: A Reader*. Chichester: John Wiley & Sons.

Lindsey, Tim. 2001. "The Criminal State: Premanisme and the New Indonesia". In *Indonesia Today: Challenges of History*, edited by Grayson Lloyd and Shannon Smith, 283–297. Lanham: Rowman and Littlefield.

Oomen, Barbara. 2004. "Vigilantism or Alternative Citizenship? The Rise of Mapogo a Mathamaga". *African Studies* 63 (2): 153–171.

Petrus, Theodore. 2015. "Enemies of the 'State': Vigilantism and the Street Gang as Symbols of Resistance in South Africa". *Aggression and Violent Behaviour* 22: 26–32.

Poskotanews.com. 2018. "Cekcok dengan preman, anggota polisi tertembak". *Poskotanews.com*, January 4, 2018. http://poskotanews.com/2018/01/04/cecok-dengan-preman-anggota-polisi-tertembak/.

Pramono, Gatot Eddy. 2015. "Transformasi Organisasi Kemasyarakatan (Ormas) Menjadi Kelompok Kekerasan (Studi kekerasan Ormas di Jakarta)". *Jurnal Keamanan Nasional* 1 (2): 251–274.

Ryter, Loren. 1998. "Pemuda Pancasila: The Last Loyalist Free Men of Suharto's Order?" *Indonesia* 66 (October): 44–73.

Schulte Nordholt, Henk. 1991. "The Jago in the Shadow. Crime and 'Order' in the Colonial State in Java". *RIMA: Review of Indonesian and Malaysian Affairs* 25 (1): 74–91.

Sen, Atreyee, and David Pratten. 2007. "Global Vigilantes: Perspectives on Justice and Violence". In *Global Vigilantes*, edited by David Pratten and Atreyee Sen, 1–24. London: Hurst Publishers.

Siegel, James. 1998. *A New Criminal Type in Jakarta: Counter-revolution Today*. Durham: Duke University Press.

Stokke, Kristian. 2017. "Politics of Citizenship: Towards an Analytical Framework". In *Politics of Citizenship in Indonesia*, edited by Eric Hiariej and Kristian Stokke, 23–54. Jakarta: Yayasan Pustaka Obor Indonesia.

Sundar, Nandini. 2010. "Vigilantism, Culpability and Moral Dilemmas". *Critique of Anthropology* 30 (1): 113–121.

Tadié, Jérôme, and Risa Permanadeli. 2015. "Night and the City: Clubs, Brothels and Politics in Jakarta". *Urban Studies* 52 (3): 471–485.

Telle, Kari. 2013. "Vigilante Citizenship: Sovereign Practices and the Politics of Insult in Indonesia". *Bijdragen tot de Taal-, Land- en Volkenkunde* 169: 183–212.

Van Klinken, Gerry. 2007. *Communal Violence and Democratization in Indonesia: Small Town Wars*. London: Routledge.

Van Stapele, Naomi. 2016. "'We Are Not Kenyans': Extra-Judicial Killings, Manhood and Citizenship in Mathare, a Nairobi Ghetto". *Conflict, Security & Development* 16 (4): 301–325.

Werbner, Richard. 2004. *Reasonable Radicals and Citizenship in Botswana: The Public Anthropology of Kalanga Elites*. Bloomington: Indiana University Press.

Wilson, Ian Douglas. 2006. "Continuity and Change. The Changing Contours of Organized Violence in Post-New Order Indonesia". *Critical Asian Studies* 38: 265–297.

Wilson, Ian Douglas. 2012. "The Biggest Cock: Territoriality, Invulnerability and Honour Amongst Jakarta's Gangsters". In *Men and Masculinities in Southeast Asia*, edited by Michelle Ford and Lenore Lyons, 121–138. London and New York: Routledge.

Wilson, Lee. 2017. "How Critical Can Critical Be? Contesting Security in Indonesia". *Critical Studies on Security* 5 (3): 302–316.

Wilson, Lee, and Laurens Bakker. 2016 "Cutting off the King's Head: Security and Normative Order Beyond the State". *Conflict, Security & Development* 16 (4): 289–300.

Wiwoho, Bimo. 2017. "Dua Sisi 'Berdamai' Dengan Preman Tanah Abang". *CNN Indonesia*, November 10, 2017. www.cnnindonesia.com/nasional/201711081510 10-32-254386/dua-sisi-berdamai-dengan-preman-tanah-abang.

4 "Loose girls bring bad boys into safe neighbourhoods"

Analysing urban security anxieties and the everyday logics of blurred moral policing in urban India

Atreyee Sen

A Monday afternoon in Chaturvadi area (in Mumbai) and two members of the Shiv Sena Mahila Aghadi, the women's wing of a powerful local Hindu nationalist party, now in power at the federal state of Maharashtra (with Mumbai as its expansive commercial capital), stepped out of their homes in a lower class colony after receiving some disturbing phone calls. They were informed that the pedestrian rail bridge connecting the East and West region of their area was yet again dotted by young couples engaged in immoral activities. The couples were kissing and hugging, but the complainants stated that matters got worse just after sunset, when they would be touching each other inappropriately. This made human traffic across the bridge difficult. Daily commuters, tired after a long day's work, had to watch these scenes of intimacy in public, or choose a longwinded route to return home. The two women were worried that young schoolgirls crossing the bridge would think it's perfectly legitimate to romance in public. "Boys will always take advantage of loose girls. How hard it must be for elderly commuters to witness such indecent behaviour from young girls. It amounts to public disrespect", one of them lamented to me scurrying after them.

On the way, they met up with two local policemen who were ready and waiting to support the women in their mission. The women party workers felt they could be nasty to the girls and scare them off, but they were concerned whether the young men would remain restrained if their girlfriends were attacked. "They might try to be macho heroes, so we need some police support", they explained. On his way to the bridge, one of the policemen removed his expensive watch. "It's a gift from my father-in-law and he will be upset if I break it while getting some lovers off a bridge. If it was lost while chasing gangsters, now that will be a good story", he laughed. The mood was light and sportive, while the four-member team marched onto the bridge. One of the Mahila Aghadi women walked up to the first couple and landed a sound slap on the girl. Just when the young boyfriend raised his hand to retaliate, one of the policemen rushed up and slapped his face. Then the team swiftly galloped towards a second couple and repeated the drill of slapping and abuse. The women smacking the girls, while the policemen threatened the boys. As one of the young couples protested, the older of the two Aghadi women grabbed the girl's mobile phone and yelled "what's your *Ai*'s (mother's) number? I am going to call her". Having realised that the women were from the Shiv Sena Mahila Aghadi and the men were plainclothes policemen, the other couples decided to sprint off. The policemen dashed after the couples while the women rubbed the sweat off their foreheads with their saris. Some people, including the anthropologist, stuck around sheepishly watching the scene, but the more bemused bystanders got busy recording the incident on their phones. The policemen returned looking satisfied after having whacked around some of the male lovers. And at the end of the show, the policemen and the Aghadi women were given a round of applause by many of the daily commuters, and the local moral task team raised their hands in acknowledgement.

Introduction

An amount of literature on neo-liberal urban growth and the management of urban spatial practices shows that policing has increasingly come to be favoured as a tool for resolving a variety of social problems. The latter may not be related to criminal and illegal activities stereotypically associated with precarious communities, but could stem from multiple conditions of marginality experienced by the urban poor (cf. Fassin 2013). This burgeoning need for armed response to even minor civil infractions produces an extensive multi-scalar securities market, which Diphoorn and Berg (2014), for example, suggest led to the birth of "partnership policing" between the public and private security industries in their study of urban South Africa. According to Samara (2010), who explored the resurgence of apartheid era policing in decrepit Cape Town housing areas, research on policing at the level of the city has focused on the role played by the police in reclaiming space, which is then reproduced through other social control mechanisms. The author (2010) suggests that these mechanisms, such as the central or business improvement districts, continue to work closely with the public and private security sectors. Many authors exploring the politics of policing in the city argue that policing organisations collaborating with the capitalist state is the source of tense relationships between the police and poor communities, contributing to a widening of urban segregation based on race, gender, class and ethnicity (cf. Samara 2010; Abrahamsen and Williams 2007; Caldeira 2002).

Some recent scholarship shows how the policing of citizens, more often than not, becomes related to negotiations with more localised power groups in global cities (cf. Purcell 2008; Hagedorn 2008). Valentine (2008), who explored the fear of gendered street crimes, suggests that the control of public space is exercised not only by the police or private security guards, but more indirectly by store managers, bus conductors, park wardens and other authorised personnel as a form of public service. This informal control of public areas is more successful in stable neighbourhoods where people have strong social and family ties through long periods of residence, and are likely to feel confident to overtly control "inappropriate" conduct within their localities (cf. Sen 2007). Studies of small-scale civil policing, violent vigilantism, mass management of communal property, and the delivering of crude justice, explores both the routinisation and brutalisation of these forms of interventions in poor neighbourhoods (cf. Radcliffe 2007; Pratten and Sen 2007; Kempa et al. 2004; Kil et al. 2009). These practices usually become more socially entrenched in the absence of state surveillance in marginalised urban areas. The latter, described by Wacquant (2007) as "cordoned off spaces", are often "left alone" by the state to manage and monitor their own systems of justice and retribution, without the investment of state resources to curtail violence and socio-economic degradation – as long as the problems embedded in these areas didn't spill over into business or gentrified districts.

This chapter complicates these strategic alliances and separations in policing actions between the state police, local administrators, private security guards, neighbourhood residents and citizen-vigilantes. I show how an overt and unconventional collaboration between low-ranked policemen, migrant security guards employed by small-scale private companies, and lower-class female civilians (such as women of the Mahila Aghadi described in the vignette above), opens up a fresh analytical space for understanding urban security blurs. The latter, in the context of my research, refers to the range of actors and actions involved in regulating the low-end, everyday politics of accessing urban public space, and in developing informal moral treatises on poor people's legitimate citizenship in the city. I also highlight how joint participation in monitoring public space not only blurs the discursive, participatory and experiential boundaries between security and insecurity (e.g. the police, the women squads and bystanders see themselves as saviours of ordinary people's safe spaces, unlike the lovers who view moral policing as the precursor to dangerous insecurities for the poor urban youth), it also leads to the clouding of gender, generational, political and professional relationships between formal and informal actors involved in the collective management of urban space.

My ethnographic landscape is mainly Mumbai: where "respectable women", ranging from right-wing activists to old ladies' groups, partnered with the neighbourhood police and security guards in lower class housing sectors, in actively cleansing public spaces of "free women". I signify this form of action as "militant moral policing" (often referred to as modesty patrol or religious police in other cultural contexts), which involves the routine, often violent, surveillance over women's dress, conduct and public display of love. I argue that the wider discourse of restrictive moral policing remains couched in the gendered language of control (of women's sexual behaviour in public), but the nuanced, micro-culture of quotidian vigilantism is designed to *protect* better access to public spaces by ordinary workers, children and the elderly. The latter are represented as the vulnerable population in the city. Their limited freedom of mobility is challenged further by the offensive display of feminine sexuality in public places. I argue that the blurred lines between multiple discourses and delivery of informal safety measures imagined and implemented through collective action, what I discuss later as joint or combined moral policing between state and non-state actors, brings into focus the importance of intimacy and morality in discussing everyday urban security practices. The fact that these practices are *not* directed towards sustaining the interests of large capitalist markets, or even servicing the securocratic state, uniquely positions this form of moral patrolling in the wider debate about policing urban spaces.

For the last two decades, I have conducted ethnographic fieldwork among poor and lower class women affiliated with the right-wing Hindu nationalist political party, the Shiv Sena, in Mumbai (cf. Sen 2006, 2007). My recent research pursuit, which relies on participant observation and in-depth interviews with the police, the lovers and women street vigilantes, explores the discursive practices around moral surveillance that has emerged among less affluent populations, mainly in response to growing concerns about sexual vulgarity in a rapidly modernising city. I will make references to select incidents of civilians involved in stripping, beating, shaming and harassment of "loose women" in other cities in India. The latter incidents were also supported by area police patrols that either overlooked or overtly participated in these confrontations. The emergence of urban moral policing is legitimised (in different religious and cultural forums) as a response to the increase in women's sexual freedoms; due to (a) the modernising impact of urban literacy and education; (b) the impact of the media and globalisation which promotes sexual choice and expression; and (c) women's overall liberation gained through their participation in the formal and shadow labour market in the city.[1] My chapter shows that this form of militant scrutiny of urban women is also intimately related to quotidian security anxieties in commercial cities in the global South. The use of public militancy, i.e. the direct deployment of threats, humiliation and shaming, a degree of physical violence, and verbal confrontations in the act of moral policing, is viewed by the women's squads as the most effective tool to deter transgressive public behaviour (unlike restrained negotiations which can rarely deter poor lovers who are desperate to seek out spaces for intimacy in the modern city). These cities have created myriad opportunities for poor, marginalised women to experiment with non-normative personal choices and public behaviour. I argue that the informal, oral and fuzzy contract between "the state (actor)" and "the (female) citizen" in controlling urban women's conduct is also related to the blurring of boundaries between insular notions of community dignity, and wider visions of danger, crime and gendered apprehensions about the loss of safe spaces in the city.

Moral policing of lovers in urban India

The control of public space is often considered to be a complex form of administrative practice that relies on various expressions of power over the movement of citizens, and the meaning and image of that space to both the people and the administrators (Schielke 2008; Sen 2017). While everyday functionality is usually presented as the paramount reason for the management of urban public space, the use and aesthetics of urban space is underpinned by modern understandings of public access and moral order. Debates surrounding the reform of urban behaviour through cultural censorship suggest that the administration of these spaces is also a reflection on the effective urban security apparatus developed by the state (cf. Atkinson 2003; Becker and Müller 2012). Even though cities in South Asia have developed open and secular settings, from civil courts to city parks, where couples can exercise choice in marriage and romance without the fear of administrative censoring, these spaces are not without cultural surveillance. My research in Mumbai shows that poor women having secret extra-marital affairs received some degree of sympathy in their localities, but young lovers kissing in public places, and young women expressing their choice of husbands, were subjected to public humiliation by a range of people, including policemen, passers-by and political groups. In many cities in India, women caught romancing by the police were often made to do sit ups while holding their ears in front of onlookers. Others were dragged by their hair through the streets, and these forms of shaming rituals were primarily designed to dissuade women from public love relationships. Most couples celebrating Valentine's Day were branded as "westoxified", and nativist political groups coordinated with the police in raiding shops, restaurants, cinema halls and shopping malls to interrupt lovers. During Valentine's Day, for example, the Hindu Mahasabha, a prominent pan-Indian Hindu nationalist organisation, instructed the police as well as its cadres to coerce Hindu couples celebrating V-day into marriage, and compel Hindu women kissing in public to either go through *shuddhikaran* (public purification ceremonies), or get married to any animal available nearby. This form of police-citizen participation in controlling modern/moral life in the city got a fair share of media attention, with journalists and film-makers mobilising public opinion against excessive surveillance of ordinary young couples.[2]

The rise of Hindu nationalism, however, became associated with more brutal "Taliban-like" moral policing against consumption of love and meat in urban centres, leading to a series of honour killings, lynching and murders.[3] News reports, documentaries and a small range of academic scholarship attempted to unpack the triumphs of urban police forces teamed with civil policing groups (often known an anti-Romeo squads, anti-Love Jihad patrols and cow vigilantes). These groups rounded up "deviants" in malls, cinemas, restaurants and shops to align them with Hindu orders of good conduct in the city (cf. Rao 2011; Bannerji 2006). While parks were emptied of couples as part of the moral cleansing of public spaces, police raids on hotels, where couples rented rooms for parties and intimacies, also came under media scrutiny. Against this backdrop of collaborative surveillance regimes in the city, this chapter shows how ordinary women, with or without affiliations with orthodox nationalist organisations, worked in partnership with (mainly) male policemen to sustain this politics of urban in/security, and persevered to establish a dominant claim over instituting moral decorum in public places. For example, I show how a female resident of a neighbourhood in suburban Mumbai used sticks to beat young girls using their community park for romantic interludes. The lower-level local police, and poor migrant security guards hired from small private companies, also took part in these patrols. All parties contended that they collectively guarded the park from potential paedophiles, kidnappers, drug-peddlers and child-traffickers acting as lovers. And they ensured that the park was safe as a children's playground in a city faced with shrinking green and open spaces. While the women needed the policemen to arrest the men as a scare tactic, the policemen relied on the women to beat the girls, an action which was outside their legal-moral jurisdiction.

This form of gendered co-dependence complicates our understanding of security blurs, as moral policing, despite being a display of conventional patriarchal authority over public morality, relies on strategic performances of security carefully crafted by both poor men and women. I eventually argue that terrorising couples "having an affair" was often intended to protect the safety of communities fairly weakened by urban economic marginalisation. "Rich girls don't need to romance on a bridge. Poor girls make themselves cheap by kissing at a pedestrian crossing in full public display. Some uncle will tell some aunty and then the whole neighbourhood will attack her poor family. Best to uproot the weed before it ruins the whole garden", said one of the policemen escorting the Mahila Aghadi women (from the introductory vignette), while slipping back his watch on his wrist. Policing of women's love affairs and limiting their immoral behaviour was directed towards pre-empting the possibility of mockery and ostracisation of lower class families, as these expulsions would escalate their precariousness in an alienating commercial city.

The big bridge

Various dimensions of urban precariousness also remained embedded within the practice of moral policing. Further discussions with the Mahila Aghadi revealed the extent to which the women within the movement felt vulnerable. Even though the Aghadi leaders could legitimise their disciplinary action as an extension of their maternal attention for young, deviant girls, they would prefer to "go it alone" only when chiding (e.g. provocatively dressed) girls walking by themselves. However, if the girls were with young men, the women, despite their political status, would fear counter assaults.

They explained to me: as women at the lowest rung of the party machinery, they did not have much political and media visibility. While senior leaders were well known through media interviews and images, ordinary women leaders hailing from the poor neighbourhoods could not wear their political affiliation as a shield. No one would recognise them beyond their own localities. So for their own safety, they needed to rely on the assistance of local policemen, who were often avid supporters of the Shiv Sena, along with being supportive neighbours. Since the policemen could not be seen attacking women in public (actions that were legally and morally unethical), they were pleased to take on the shared talk of moral policing and only strike young men. They would have probably done the same to their own sons, they said. According to the Aghadi leaders, this variety of collaborative moral policing carried enormous parental authority. Thus the threat of reporting to the mother, as discussed in the introductory vignette, was designed to remind the young lovers that their parents were the carriers of culture in their families. Irresponsible public behaviour would be an embarrassment to these cultural anchors. This form of emotional blackmailing guaranteed the quick exit of the couples, which left the streets safe for unconstrained human traffic for a few days.

While chatting later with the policemen, I discovered how moral policing was represented as an extension of their social duty. The men admitted that it was not illegal, but only immoral to romance on the bridge; so they needed the support of older Aghadi women with moral authority to successfully take up the task of evicting couples. The policemen suggested that their reputation as corrupt, lower class men, who often asked young couples for bribes and allowed them to use public toilets for sex, was easily salvaged when they aligned themselves with moral task forces. "This is good security", said one of the policemen. During the course of my research, I met a number of policemen who collaborated with local Mahila Aghadi leaders and cadres. The men felt that moral policing was a small effort. It was low cost and low investment, but it pre-empted criminalisation of certain localities. The presence of lovers attracted drug-sellers, pimps, brokers for cheap hotel rooms, alcohol-peddlers and a host of other criminals trying to make a profit from public areas used by couples for pleasure and hedonism. The policemen also showed me extensive case files involving couples arrested for having sex in public ("hauling and pulling", was a common English term used in the arrest reports). Some cases were concerned with sexual predators seducing young girls in public places, and later forcing them into prostitution. There were many cases of young men who were so sexually aroused while romancing in the public spaces, that they raped their innocent girlfriends "on the spot". Or they later sexually abused and assaulted other women in parks, after their girlfriends had returned home. And then there were stories of men masturbating in public spaces after having spent time with their lovers kissing and cuddling. Both the policemen and the Aghadi women felt that good women do have a "right to the city" (*unko haq hain*).

Even though moral policing was related to controlling women's behaviour, it was not directly associated with curbing *all* women's mobility. Controlling the behaviour of "loose women" meant that hard-working, decent, moral and respectable women and their families could use public space with a sense of security, without the fear of encountering urban criminality. From the perspective of the local, protectionist political party, and the policemen, the role of public service meant keeping public spaces accessible to "the decent poor". The policemen stated how "dirty activities" also occurred in hotels and motels, but organising raids and arrests required more resources. Two hours a day, with just two policemen, was a cheap and effective way to control public indecency, and boost the quality of urban mobility.

A number of policemen argued that they were fairly protected by the random "stop and search" provision in police law, and did not fear a backlash against their policing activities on the bridge. The Criminal Penal Code does empower the police to stop and search a person for any "reasonable suspicion". However, scholars argue that despite community police stations in the Mumbai slums (which offers opportunities for poor people to access police resources), local people still remain suspicious of the Bombay Police Act, which makes permissible all kinds of police harassment done in the name of public service (cf. Roy et al. 2004). Thus, the standard of "reasonable suspicion", was further diluted by the caveat introduced by the Bombay Police Act, that searches done in "good faith" were legitimate, regardless of the manner of their execution (cf. Belur 2010, 2011). Thus, public surveillance operations were not subject to any significant legal or departmental scrutiny, unlike the systemic review that similar police operations received in the Anglo-American context (ibid.). According to Belur (2011), who studies the politics of these stop and search operations among the Mumbai Police, these forms of patrolling were expressions of both control and reassurance. While it exhibited the police's capacity to exercise its authority, it also showed how the urgency of controlling crime was experienced equally by the police and the public. The author argues that these performances of stop and search operations were framed as a theatre, where the act of giving safety to people in designated areas remained a transparent attempt to gain public confidence (ibid.). Given this legal and political landscape (the Shiv Sena being in power), the police were fairly satisfied claiming high operational success when chasing young lovers off a bridge. According to Reid (2009), who explored the patterns of global urban policing, these kinds of dramatic police interventions comfort the public because of their spectacular visibility. However, most hardened criminals in Mumbai commit offences well outside the remit of small-scale moral policing. As a superficial "situational crime prevention intervention", the effectiveness of safeguarding urban public spaces through joint moral policing, remained limited to lower-level policemen "having done a good deed for the day".

This celebration of moral policing as a good deed was embodied in the non-intervention of bystanders. It was a form of covert sympathy for the collaborative effort between citizens and state actors, but it was also an enjoyment of what my informants call "mild violence". I had a few conversations with couples that often returned to the bridge, even after being humiliated on several occasions. They did not have access to clubs, upper class cafes, and private rooms to experiment with sex, intimacy and love. They told me how the bridge was shaded, there were places to sit and lean against, which made romancing easier during the summer and monsoon seasons. The pedestrian bridges were also equidistant from the residences of young lovers, and were a convenient place to meet and cuddle before heading back home after school or university. All couples resented the attacks.

The girls however were more terrified of being "formally arrested" and taken to local police stations, where they would have felt defenceless in police lock-ups. Even though the couples were vulnerable to moral policing, and to other criminals posing as lovers, the height over the city offered a nice view so the bridge remained a romantic hotspot. Watching veteran lovers using the spot usually encouraged shy couples to become more bold and intimate. "Bollywood movies show how lovers meet or part ways on a bridge", one of the boys told me, looking rather sad that he might not be able to return to "their spot" after a recent spate of moral policing. He mentioned how pedestrian streets had people, stall owners and hawkers, so there was no place to talk. Because of the potentially unhurried nature of human traffic on the streets, people would also stare and jeer at couples. However, the pedestrian bridge usually had people rushing around to catch a train or get home; so with a constantly moving flow of people, the couples felt safe enough to experience privacy in a crowded area. The people only stopped to watch when the moral policing started.

Joint moral policing generated multiple notions of urban safety and urban victimologies from the perspectives of all parties involved, whether as victims, instigators and perpetrators. These victimologies foreground the notion of security blurs, as they highlight the multi-discursivity embedded in various actions related to the power of security practices. I have shown how informal and oral contracts between state actors and citizens (the policemen whether on or off duty were also sympathetic to the cause of moral policing) created and expanded spaces and practices related to multiple understandings of urban security. All the groups involved in these policing encounters were ordinary members of lower class and poorly paid urban communities (policemen, lower class Aghadi women and young lovers), who did not have access to the city through the trappings of affluence and privilege. Holston (2009), who studies conflicts specific to entanglements of urban citizenship, argues that "insurgent citizenships" or clashes over alternative formulations of citizenship in the city are not merely idiosyncratic or instrumental protest. He states that insurgent urban citizenships may usurp central civic space and even overrun the centre, but they are fundamentally manifestations of peripheries. The author argues: "It is an insurgence that begins with the struggle for the right to have a daily life in the city worthy of a citizen's dignity" (2009, 246).

Following and twisting his strain of thought, I argue that lower class women and ordinary policemen's desire to establish their sovereignty over public space (framing their protest against young lovers in terms of rights to the elderly, the children and the respectable poor; in terms of motherhood, parenthood, justice, fear of further marginalisation and segregation; and in terms of decorum and decency), entrenches and legitimises their presence in the organisation of that space. While the women vigilantes and the policemen view the modernising city spawning emancipatory, gendered cultures as a bane for the urban poor; security discourses, which are also fundamentally a product of modern urbanity, allows upholders of collaborative moral security practices to return themselves to the city as worthy and non-peripheral citizens. The following ethnographic snippet shows further how insurgent varieties of moral cleansing becomes related to the autonomy of the lower classes, not just in prominent public spaces but also in smaller community areas which remain vital to "the outdoor lives" of peripheral neighbourhoods.

A small park

There were two traffic constables who stood below the window of an elderly woman resident in a lower middle class housing estate in suburban Mumbai. They called out to Radhatai (80), who came out of her small one-bed apartment with a wooden stick. Along with the two constables she marched to a small park in the middle of the housing colony. Without much ado, she started beating (with a frail hand) all the young lovers sitting on the park benches. The park was crumbling, and a large section of it was covered in mud and sand. There were a couple of children's swings and slides embedded in the muddy area. In the little green patch, there were a few benches, and a broken fountain covered with fungus and slime. While Radhatai was chasing away the young couples, the two traffic constables yelled at them waving their small police batons in the air. "You take rest now" said one of them kindly to Radhatai, who sat at the edge of the fountain to catch her breath. She went on to explain to me, that she needed the two policemen to help her. She was too fragile to do this work by herself, and the men in the locality "found it embarrassing to take on the task of chasing away couples from the local park", she said. The policemen on the other hand stated that Radhatai had a strong status within the community as a respectable widow, and since they were constables in this area for a long time, they had a good relationship with her. They do "this work" out of respect for her, and also because they have little to do in the early evenings. However, Radhatai made it clear to me that this duty to "clear" the park during sunset was important, as children came home from school and needed a place to play. It was also the time when the air got cooler, and elderly members of the housing colony could sit on the benches for a chat and gossip. She didn't want the park to be inaccessible to people from the colony because the lovers, both straight and queer, were occupying that precious little space.

The park was small and there were only a few lovers, so Radhatai did not make a case for drug dealers and sexual predators. She, along with a significant number of people in the housing colony, felt that lovers in smaller parks attracted peeping toms and pornographic photographers who used these images for public and personal use. Even if a couple was "innocent", the presence of young couples in their park hauled in the nefarious "others" who would exploit the freedom of love in public. This would eventually make the park area dangerous for local residents. "Loose girls bring bad boys into safe neighbourhoods", said Radhatai. Photos of couples in indecent poses would eventually end up either on the Internet, or for public ridicule in the hands of the urban underbelly. Some of the older women in the neighbourhood represented themselves as guardian angels of the area, but because of their age, they felt compelled to coordinate with the local traffic constables, as well as local security guards employed through private companies.

The security guards, who usually came into Mumbai from rural or peri-urban areas, were often quite shocked to see lovers kissing in the park. They were employed to guard the entrance gates of these small housing colonies, but were not trained security professionals in uniform that were employed by affluent housing sectors. Usually recruited through familiar kinship networks, which introduced them to smaller security firms, the guards felt that participating in these "chasing" actions with Radhatai enabled them to build trust in the housing colony. For example, Raju, a migrant from Bihar, was apprehensive about the bad reputation of security guards. Especially after the rising numbers of rape and murders of single, working women by migrant security staff in Mumbai and other cities in India. Raju offered to do groceries and helped Radhatai with many other tasks, including paying electricity and water bills. He suggested to me that his relationship with Radhatai was not purely instrumental, in that he was not just using her prominence in the neighbourhood to gain job security. He genuinely respected her work to keep the locality free of morally corrupt women. He reiterated that chasing away these women didn't mean that he wanted to harm them, and that's why he needed Radhatai as a front to give his actions some legitimacy. "Did she ask you to join her?" I asked. "No, but other men in the neighbourhood said she is old, give her a hand. They found 'lover-removal' an awkward thing to do", he said.

My ethnography shows how moral policing creates a quotidian intimacy between state and civil society members, related to love, respect and mutual affection for the locality. Unlike the Shiv Sena women, who couched their policing in the language of "morality", Radhatai's account was clearly related to a spatial battle, her desire for a safe neighbourhood, and her dependence on local police and security men in the absence of other male support. The nature of moral policing in big and small public spaces, in major junctions and enclosed residential areas, showed that the form of policing, often led by women, was not directly related to achieving or abetting state power. Even though there may be a period of political incubation, when the leading nationalist party learns to directly support violent activities by moral citizens, the hegemonic discourse around moral policing remained closely tied to the authority of the good, moral but poor citizen, over those sections of the urban population blindly seduced by the negative accoutrements of urban modernity. This was not a static state of domination, but a process of reproduction of urban values, which reorganised urban culture and society.

Police and policing women

According to Pain (2001), different notions of femininity are entwined with constructions of the fear of public spaces; many authors like her suggest that the emphasis on dread and distress produce and reproduce feminine weakness in public. For example, this weakness generates what Koskela (1997) refers to as a tension between gendered spatial confidence, bold walking, and spatial avoidance in many urban cultural contexts. Stanko (1996) and Bradford et al. (2009), while exploring the complex relationship between women and crime, suggest that these fears are more dramatically entrenched, when women identify the police and members of security agencies not as protectors, but as sources of threat. According to Jauregui (2013), who investigates the ways in which the Indian police force developed a poor reputation, members of the police who work at the lowest level serve as "whipping boys" for society's greater ills. She notes further that the news and entertainment media, as well as other modes of public culture, broadly portray the police either as incompetent fools, as little more than "yes men" to more powerful figures, or as brutal and corrupt "little tyrants" (2013, 645). The lower-ranking police in India, constables and sub-inspectors, who constitute more than 90 percent of the police force in each state, are a despised minority, especially in the absence of meaningful police reform in the post-colonial period (ibid.). In the limited amount of literature that addresses questions of police legitimacy in India – the institution has been described as a crumbling edifice, and as manifesting a systemic rot in Indian governance (ibid.). Even among the police, there was widespread lack of faith in the institution, and the notion of the "honest cop" was considered a myth (ibid.). Social media and other progressive news channels often reported police indifference to women's complaints of sexual harassment in public, and how degenerate policemen raped, attacked and locked away women who approached them for help.

I have shown how the policemen attempted to redeem their pathetic image by supporting older women's crusades against moral indecency in the city. However, the policemen who interrupted intimacy and struck young lovers in public also urged young women to imagine themselves as complicit in a (moral) crime. And they made them terrified of the consequences of being arrested by corrupt and sexually degenerate policemen with no respect for "loose women". I argue that the notorious reputation of the police force became a weapon to tackle the sexual and spatial confidence of young women, and the monitoring of wider public security became a ruse for challenging the everyday security of women deemed as immoral sexual invaders within the cityscape.

According to Waddington et al. (2004), who explored the ways in which the police forces patrol the boundaries of inclusion/exclusion, humiliating encounters with policemen had the possibility to undermine the freedom and status of those who persevered to reconceptualise public space as an equal sphere for the marginalised. Even though the police attempted to develop a sacred image as a coterie of people with monopoly on legitimate violence, the non-criminalised population that had violent contact with the police found it highly unsettling (ibid.). In Kolkata, a city in eastern India, in a case of public sexual harassment (which received an amount of media attention in the city), the victim did not receive any support from the police despite having identified her attackers as members of a prominent political party. She was openly desisted from writing a complaint, and was finally asked to rewrite her complaint several times to give her an opportunity to retract her report.[4] Many other urban centres were criticised by the media for allowing the police and the local moral police to work closely towards curbing the use of public space for personal pleasure. I would argue further that this decline in trust in the police not only created gender segregated urban spaces and movements, the authority exercised by the police in creating an asymmetrical relationship between the police and deviant users of public space, also blurred the notion of public safety for *all* women; the latter could be random targets, since the boundaries of moral policing remained complex and flexible, and could encompass any women at any time. Having said that, moral policing viewed through the lens of everyday commuters, poor women workers, and the elderly, was an effective form of "community engagement". Increase in patrol activity (as yet) was viewed as a trust-building exercise, rather than as a detriment to fair access to public space.

According to Phadke (2007), who studies women's access to public spaces in Mumbai, and Marrow (2013), who explores sexual vulnerability among women using public space in urban India, ordinary people's ideas of everyday risk determine women's legitimate claim to public space. Phadke (2007) argues that safety is linked directly to the level of claim that one *feels* to a space. "It is more than the promise of not being physically harmed", she states (2007, 1511), it includes the knowledge that female citizens can be incorporated into urban living to such an extent that their presence in the public space should not be looked at askance. While "paranoid parenting" of girl children create gendered and racialised geographies of risk, where paedophiles and asylum seekers increasingly replace the "stranger" in girl children's accounts of danger (cf. Pain 2006), women's sense of anxiety, risk and mobility has been globally manufactured and managed through the fear of assault in public. This impacts women's understanding of using public space as both a right and a benefit. Community squares, residential parks and pedestrian crossings are spaces that emphasise recognition. Social encounters in these spaces are relatively frequent, informal and can quickly become familiar through repeated visits. While lovers in parks may view these spaces as purposeful "micro-publics", the politics of urban security make these open spaces vulnerable, stressful and replete with experiences of discrimination. However, young women who regularly use public squares for romance do not expect assaults from other women, and rarely identify other women as risk. This chapter has shown how older women exercise their right to control the bodies and presence of disorderly women in public. By diminishing the visibility of women who challenge conventional moral expression of feminine behaviour, older women involved in moral policing enhance their own visibility as protectors of urban space.

Despite the proliferation of moral policing in many urban centres in India, there has also been significant resistance from the youth. Students have held mass protests against moral surveillance. Many young people have openly displayed their solidarity for the "kiss of love" campaign, which attempted to build a pan-Indian alliance against the suppression of sexuality in public.[5] My point is that women on both sides of the moral policing debate engage with the notion of risk with originality, and they do articulate their demands with physical and emotional force, with a toehold to a rhetoric or campaign about women, freedom and public security. In the process of defending their right to use public and commuter spaces, the women, the young lovers, and the policemen, get involved in creating different orders of citizenship in the city.

Concluding comments: exploring security blurs

My analysis has contributed to the debate on security blurs by underlining the ways in which the notion remains complex and multi-layered in the milieus of urban marginalities. Security blurs in the context of moral policing in Mumbai highlights the blurring of *actors* and *actions* related to what the editors define as the manifestations of security that are visible and identifiable. Informal policing actions involve lower class women, lower-level policemen, and poor migrant security guards who take part in the everyday, physical cleansing of crime and crime-related activities in public spaces accessed by the urban poor. It also leads to the blurring of *gender* and *generational* aspects of security practices, as women use violence, threats, seniority and patriarchal authority to monitor public spaces, which have been historically used and recognised locally as a masculinist space. The male policemen and security guards engage with mild violence, display "dim heroism" (unlike the bright valour of catching a real criminal, as lamented by the policeman in the introductory vignette), and collaborate with ordinary women's collectives, in order to make the project of delivering security, which involves ousting young women from public space, a success. The concept of security blurs also allows us to understand the *discursive opportunities* created by moral policing; in offering visibility to marginalised right-wing and elderly women, to policemen mocked and accused of corruption, to security guards with a reputation for theft and murder, and to lovers gallantly resisting coercion. Eventually, security blurs expand the notion of insecurity. Moral policing legitimised as a response to a crisis in *spatial security*, becomes intimately related economic insecurity, predicaments in the good use of leisure spaces, "correct" access of public space by poor urban citizens, and political insecurity among lower class nationalist women. Forms of "extreme blurring" are neatly articulated in the ethnographic section on the management of a decrepit park by a small locality: where resident men inhibited to police lovers, outsource moral policing to distrustful security guards and elderly women, and local police constables with reverential sentiments towards local elderly women, join the latter in small-scale spatial cleansing. The elderly women who are too frail to carry out security actions recruit the support of these lower class men, and use the morally superior discursive position of creating crime-free areas for poor children, to dislodge poor lovers from their free spaces. I reiterate that these blurs can become routinised enactments of everyday security when actors, agents, actions, gendered discourses, experiences of crime and crisis related to moral policing, merge and flow into each other in the ordinary lives of the urban poor.

Studies of security and its relationship to urban landscapes have a long history in the social sciences. In recent years, researchers have come to offer increasingly nuanced investigations of urban violence, questioning how they highlight the uneven patterns of urban poverty and growth that characterise so many commercial cities, especially in the global South. In this chapter, I have attempted to show the importance of ethnographic research that can account for the ways that violence and security are embodied and experienced in everyday urban space. These experiences, pertaining to the differing effects that management of public spaces produce within bodies, raises an ethnographic question: how can we reflect on blurred securities in the city when poor women (with some political and generational power) attack poor and lower class men and women (with some educational and economic power) with the help of poor men (with some legal and administrative power)? From the effect of being shamed in public, to larger economic and political shifts that accompany forms of moral policing, the geographies of gender require subtlety in order to see the multitudinous relationships that exist within debates on security and the use of public space. Accounting for these specificities allows scholars to recognise that the blurring of lines between discourses and delivery of in/formal security are central to understanding broader patterns of violence and gendered mobility, as they increasingly collide with processes of urban change. As urbanisation steadily encompasses ever more people throughout the developing world, it becomes important to comprehend how the politics of policing shed light on the ways that people experience small and big spaces in the city; and how these encounters create temporary and bleary interpretations of urban security from the perspective of both victims and persecutors of violence. These forms of inclusion and exclusion from urban space impact spatio-temporal milieus, and eventually develop gendered geographies of urban fear.

Notes

1 www.huffingtonpost.in/news/moral-policing/
2 www.thehindu.com/news/national/other-states/hindu-mahasabha-takes-aim-at-valentines-day/article6853822.ece
3 www.telegraph.co.uk/news/2017/04/02/fears-india-spread-taliban-like-moral-policing-amid-crackdown/
4 www.huffingtonpost.in/2016/04/19/kolkata_0_n_9725636.html
5 https://timesofindia.indiatimes.com/city/bengaluru/Bengaluru-Kiss-of-Love-plan-sets-off-protest/articleshow/45197732.cms

References

Abrahamsen, Rita, and Michael C. Williams. 2007. "Securing the City: Private Security Companies and Non-state Authority in Global Governance". *International Relations* 21: 237–253.

Atkinson, Rowland. 2003. "Domestication by Cappuccino or a Revenge on Urban Space? Control and Empowerment in the Management of Public Spaces". *Urban Studies* 40 (9): 1829–1843.

Bannerji, Himani. 2006. "Making India Hindu and Male: Cultural Nationalism and the Emergence of the Ethnic Citizen in Contemporary India". *Ethnicities* 6 (3): 362–390.

Becker, Anne, and Markus-Michael Müller. 2012. "The Securitization of Urban Space and the 'Rescue' of Downtown Mexico City". *Vision and Practice* 40 (2): 77–94.

Belur, Jyoti. 2010. *Permission to Shoot? Police Use of Deadly Force in Democracies.* New York: Springer.

Belur, Jyoti. 2011. "Police Stop and Search in India: Mumbai *Nakabandi*". *Policing and Society* 21 (4): 420–431.

Bradford, Ben, Jonathan Jackson, and Elizabeth A. Stanko. 2009. "Contact and Confidence: Revisiting the Impact of Public Encounters With the Police". *Policing and Society* 19 (1): 20–46.

Caldeira, Teresa. 2002. "The Paradox of Police Violence in Democratic Brazil". *Ethnography* 3 (3): 235–263.

Diphoorn, Tessa, and Julie Berg. 2014. "Typologies of Partnership Policing: Case Studies from Urban South Africa". *Policing and Society* 24 (4): 425–442.

Fassin, Didier. 2013. *Enforcing Order: An Ethnography of Urban Policing.* Cambridge: Polity Press.

Hagedorn, John. 2008. *A World of Gangs: Armed Young Men and Gangsta Culture.* Minneapolis: University of Minnesota Press.

Holston, James. 2009. "Insurgent Citizenship in an Era of Global Urban Peripheries". *City & Society* 21 (2): 245–267.

Jauregui, Beatrice. 2013. "Beatings, Beacons, and Big Men: Police Disempowerment and Delegitimation in India". *Law & Social Inquiry* 38 (3): 643–669.

Kempa, Michael, Philip Stenning, and Jennifer Wood. 2004. "Policing Communal Spaces: A Reconfiguration of the 'Mass Private Property' Hypothesis". *The British Journal of Criminology* 44 (4): 562–581.

Kil, Sang H., Cecilia Menjívar, and Roxanne L. Doty. 2009. "Securing Borders: Patriotism, Vigilantism and the Brutalization of the US American Public". In *Immigration, Crime and Justice (Sociology of Crime, Law and Deviance, Volume 13)*, edited by William F. Mcdonald, 297–312. Bingley: Emerald Group Publishing.

Koskela, Hille. 1997. "'Bold Walk and Breakings': Women's Spatial Confidence Versus Fear of Violence". *Gender, Place & Culture* 4 (3): 301–320.

Marrow, Jocelyn. 2013. "Feminine Power or Feminine Weakness? North Indian Girls' Struggles with Aspirations, Agency, and Psychosomatic Illness". *American Ethnologist* 40 (2): 347–361.

Pain, Rachel. 2001. "Gender, Race, Age and Fear in the City". *Urban Studies* 38 (5–6): 899–913.

Pain, Rachel. 2006. "Paranoid Parenting? Rematerializing Risk and Fear for Children". *Social & Cultural Geography* 7 (2): 221–243.

Phadke, Shilpa. 2007. "Dangerous Liaisons: Women and Men: Risk and Reputation in Mumbai". *Economic and Political Weekly* 42 (17): 1510–1518.

Pratten, David, and Atreyee Sen, eds. 2007. *Global Vigilantes*. London: C. Hurst and Co.

Purcell, Mark. 2008. *Recapturing Democracy: Neoliberalization and the Struggle for Alternative Urban Futures*. New York: Routledge.

Radcliffe, Sarah A. 2007. "Latin American Indigenous Geographies of Fear: Living in the Shadow of Racism, Lack of Development, and Antiterror Measures". *Annals of the Association of American Geographers* 97 (2): 385–397.

Rao, Mohan. 2011. "Love Jihad and Demographic Fears". *Indian Journal of Gender Studies* 18 (3): 425–430.

Reid, Kiron. 2009. "Race Issues and Stop-and-Search: Looking Behind the Statistics". *The Journal of Criminal Law* 73: 165–183.

Roy, Ash Narian, Arputham Jockin, and Ahmad Javed. 2004. "Community Police Stations in Mumbai's Slums". *Environment and Urbanization* 16 (2): 135–138.

Samara, Tony Roshan. 2010. "Policing Development: Urban Renewal as Neo-liberal Security Strategy". *Urban Studies* 47 (1): 197–214.

Schielke, Samuli. 2008. "Policing Ambiguity: Muslim Saints-day Festivals and the Moral Geography of Public Space in Egypt". *American Ethnologist* 35 (4): 539–552.

Sen, Atreyee. 2006. "Reflecting on Resistance: Hindu Women 'Soldiers' Remember the Birth of Female Militancy". *Indian Journal of Gender Studies* 13 (1): 1–35.

Sen, Atreyee. 2007. *Shiv Sena Women: Violence and Communalism in a Bombay Slum*. London: C. Hurst and Co.

Sen, Atreyee. 2017. "Sumitai, the Vigilante in a Mumbai Slum". *Terrain: Journal of Ethnology, Social and Cultural Anthropology*. http://terrain.revues.org/16247.

Stanko, Elizabeth. 1996. "Warnings to Women: Police Advice and Women's Safety in Britain". *Violence Against Women* 2: 5–24.

Valentine, Gill. 2008. "Living with Difference: Reflections on Geographies of Encounter". *Progress in Human Geography* 32 (3): 323–337.

Wacquant, Lois. 2007. *Urban Outcasts: A Comparative Sociology of Advanced Marginality*. Cambridge: Polity.

Waddington, Peter A.J., Kevin Stenson, and David Don. 2004. "Race, and Police Stop-and-Search". *British Journal of Criminology* 44: 889–914.

5 Disputed sovereignty

Entanglements of state and civilian policing in Maputo, Mozambique

Helene Maria Kyed

Introduction

This chapter explores everyday policing in a crime-ridden, poorer area of Maputo, Mozambique and discusses the various security blurs that occur in the overlaps, entanglements and cooperation between state police officers and civilian policing actors. In that context, I argue, we need to understand security blurs not simply as benevolent forms of complementarity and hybridity in legally plural contexts, but as deeply political. In everyday performances and interactions between state and civilian policing actors this politics is evident in subtle competition over power, benefits and legitimacy. At a structural level, security blurs in Maputo are conditioned by a general situation of disputed or uncertain sovereignty as well as by the insecurities that characterise life in poor neighbourhoods. I base these claims on long-term ethnographic fieldwork among state police officers and civilian community policing agents inside a Maputo neighbourhood, which I call Chasana, and at the police station, that covers Chasana and ten other *barrios* (neighbourhoods).[1]

The civilian policing agents that I followed were predominantly young men from poorer families who started to voluntarily engage in policing activities after the Ministry of Interior piloted a community-policing programme in 2001. Officially, this programme aimed to enhance collaboration between the state police and citizens by establishing Community Policing Councils (MINT 2005). The intention was never to allow civilians to substitute for and act like the state police, but in practice this was largely what happened in places like Chasana. While never officially endorsed, the civilian agents became both the extended arm of and a competitor to the police.

In this chapter, I first illustrate how the policing roles of the civilian agents and state police officers constantly blurred through mutual interdependencies, entanglements and exchanges. The civilian agents performed functions legally confined to the state police, like arrests, investigations and apprehension of stolen goods, and state police officers extensively relied on the civilian agents to boost their capacity to act inside the neighbourhood. Each set of actors relied on each other to assert authority, gain protection and reap benefits. Importantly, this blurring of policing actors predominantly revolved around informalised policing practices where the shared purpose of security provision, for civilian and state policing actors alike, was to resolve disputes and crimes *outside* state legal procedures. The resolution practices drew on a locally familiar domain of community-based justice, applied by elders and community leaders, but these were combined with techniques, artefacts and languages that people in Chasana associated with the state (Hansen and Stepputat 2001) (e.g. the use of stamps, law references, registers, police titles, physical torture, batons, cells and handcuffs). State aspects were integrative parts of informal policing. Therefore, what I observed was both a blurring of types of policing actors and of types of order-making practices. As I show with an ethnographic case study of a mobile theft, such blurriness was partly influenced by the victims' demands for immediate and compensational justice. Informalised policing simultaneously involved physical torture and extraction of rewards, which were familiar, yet illegal aspects of state policing in Maputo.

These performative security blurs did not however erase differences or efforts to establish hierarchies and distinctions between civilian and state policing actors. In the second part of the chapter, I illustrate how blurriness co-existed with different forms of boundary-making that revolved around competition over power, benefits and legitimacy. While state police officers extensively relied on the civilian agents, they did not accept it when their civilian counterparts acted in ways that made them appear too much like the state police. This was most apparent when the civilian agents received a police-like uniform, as I show with a second ethnographic case. Boundary-making was also apparent when the civilian agents acted autonomously from the police officers and tried to get official recognition or enter the police college. In such situations, the police officers tried to position themselves as superior. Although they relied on civilian agents to assert authority in the neighbourhoods, this reliance needed to be confined to the informal realm of policing or it would challenge the state police's *de jure* sovereign power.

At a deeper level of analysis, as I address in the conclusion to the chapter, this ambiguous relationship, oscillating between collaboration and competition, and between entanglements and boundary-making, reflects that security blurs are shaped by a wider political context where sovereignty has historically remained disputed as no particular set of actors *de facto* hold a sovereign position to make order (Kyed and Albrecht 2015). This uncertain sovereignty is exacerbated by the high insecurity that prevails in poorer urban neighbourhoods like Chasana where people mistrust state legal procedures and prefer immediate justice. The flipside of security blurs in such contexts, I conclude, is the central role that violence plays in asserting positions of power and in overcoming uncertainty. In drawing these conclusions I add to the theories on legal pluralism (Santos 2006; Griffiths 1986; Merry 1988), plural policing (Baker 2002; Wood and Shearing 2007), and the political anthropological approach to sovereignty (Hansen and Stepputat 2005; Comaroff and Comaroff 2006; Gazit 2009; Bertelsen 2016; Kyed and Albrecht 2015), which I discuss in the next section before I return to Chasana.

Sovereignty and pluralism

Most studies of security and justice provision in Mozambique have applied theories of legal pluralism (Santos 2006; Trindade and Santos 2003; Araújo 2009; Kyed et al. 2012; Kyed 2007; Meneses 2004). By recognising the existence of more than one set of binding rules within a social field, the concept of legal pluralism provides a non-state centric and non-legalistic approach that allows for other norms and actors than those associated with the state to be included within definitions of law and order making (Griffiths 1986; Merry 1988). Santos (2006), in addition argues that legal pluralism in contemporary Mozambique is not equal to the co-existence of distinct legal systems, such as state versus traditional or community-based. Instead there are multiple overlaps and combinations of norms and practices within and between state, traditional and communal arrangements. To describe these combinations, Santos (2006) applies the concepts of "hybridisation" and "interlegality". These resonate well with the kinds of security blurs that I observed in the entanglements between state and civilian policing actors in Chasana. However, whereas Santos (2006, 45) recognises "conflicts and tensions between different legal orders", his focus is on the forms of complementarity and mutual influences that develop from hybridisation. This focus omits a deeper consideration of those ongoing forms of competition and power struggles that occur between various justice and security actors as they try to assert authority or defend a particular order, as Tamanaha (2008) has equally argued. The significant role that violence often plays in plural policing contexts, such as Chasana, is equally overlooked. A similar omission can be found in the newer literature on plural policing, which has provided tremendously useful insights into the ways that state, communal and private policing actors, rationalities and practices overlap, enrol and oppose each other in post-colonial contexts (Wood and Shearing 2007; Abrahamsen and Williams 2009; Baker 2002). Drawing on a Foucauldian-inspired conception of power, this literature concludes that plural policing gives way to security arrangements where there is no clear-cut centre of authority and no fixed hierarchical relationships (Abrahamsen and Williams 2009). Power is diffused rather than concentrated in particular institutions. While my insights from Chasana confirm that the state police do not hold a monopoly on the power to make order, but works through and in competition with civilian agents, I also show that a too strong emphasis on the diffusions of power risks losing sight of the simultaneously observable enactments of boundaries, hierarchies and claims to superior authority. To capture these forms of boundary-making, and their violent expressions, I suggest, like Bertelsen (2016, 248–249) who explores state formation in central Mozambique, to add to the legal pluralism and plural policing literatures a focus on contested and multiple sovereignty.

Inspired by political anthropological studies, I approach sovereign power not alone as vested in *de jure* state sovereignty, but as a set of practices concerned with claims to superior authority, the legitimate use of force and the making of final decisions on punishments (see Hansen and Stepputat 2005; Comaroff and Comaroff 2006; Gazit 2009). These sovereign enactments can occur *outside* the official law and state institutions as more or less localised expressions of sovereign power within the informal realms of for instance neighbourhood policing. In Chasana, police officers constantly asserted power by referring to official state law, but *de facto* operated *outside* it and thus both took part in making and suspending the law (Benjamin 1978, 287). The civilian agents did much the same, but without the backing of *de jure* state sovereignty. Conversely, the contestations over sovereign power between state police and civilian agents were mediated by popular demands for immediate and tangible justice in contradiction to formal legal processes. Exploring sovereignty in this way challenges the monolithic, state-centric and absolutist aspects of national sovereignty, emphasising instead the fragmented and non-finite aspects of sovereign power in post-colonies and poor urban areas like Chasana (Bertelsen 2016, 253). Rather than substituting the absolutist notion of sovereignty with one of benign pluralism and uncontested diffusion of power, the emphasis is rather on the existence of a multiplicity of "more or less effective claim[s] on part of any agent, community, cadre, or collective to exercise autonomous, exclusive control" (Comaroff and Comaroff 2006, 35). This perspective allows us to capture the simultaneous blurring of security with always momentary and contested efforts to centralise and consolidate power within certain institutions and bodies. In contrast to Bertelsen (2016), I do not argue for the irrelevance of concepts like pluralism and hybridisation, but rather view these as existing in a productive tension with different forms of boundary-making and enactments of sovereign power (Kyed 2017d).

In the following, I begin with the forms of blurred security that occurred in practice in Chasana, followed by a discussion of the boundary-making that simultaneously infused the relationship between state police officers and the civilian policing agents.

From official community policing to everyday security blurs

In the mid-1990s, Chasana was one of those low-income neighbourhoods on the outskirts of the inner city of Maputo that became notorious for high levels of violent crime and street-level assaults, which were the result of rising youth unemployment and lack of adequate policing. This was at the beginning of the democratic transition, which followed the end of 16 years of civil war. Despite high levels of growth, job-creation was low and although efforts were made to democratise the public sector, including the police, it was simultaneously downsized. Along with corruption and prioritisation of elite interests, these developments left neighbourhoods like Chasana with meagre public security provision and with growing incidences of popular lynching of criminals (Serra 2008).

It was this situation that motivated a General, heading the public relations department within the Ministry of Interior, to adopt a community-policing programme in 2001. While the programme was clearly inspired by international models, which emphasise police accountability and responsiveness to citizen needs, including a reduction of police violations of human rights (see Brogden and Nijhar 2005), the intention in Mozambique was also that community-police partnerships would enable the state police to (re)gain sway over criminalised neighbourhoods. This programme came after almost a decade of post-war police reform, which squarely focused on professionalising the state police in accordance with the rule of law, but which in practice failed to curb rising urban crime, reduce state police corruption and violence, and decrease widespread mistrust between state police and citizens (Kyed 2017c; Baker 2002). Community policing was officially promoted as a solution to these failures. Through the establishment of "community policing councils", it was intended to enhance collaboration between the state police and selected community members in solving problems of crime and in reducing police misconduct (MINT 2005).[2] Simultaneously, a sector police officer from the police stations was posted inside every neighbourhood to support police-community partnerships. Apart from allowing civilians to do neighbourhood patrols and mediate minor disputes, the Ministry of Interior never intended the community-policing programme to allow civilians to substitute for and act like the state police. In practice, however, this is largely what happened in places like Chasana. One unintended effect was that the reliance on civilians to strengthen the state police simultaneously empowered civilians to act like a police force, yet within an informalised realm of policing.

When I began fieldwork in 2009, there was a widespread belief that community policing had reduced violent crime, although youth unemployment was still high. This change was accredited not to a formal community policing council, however, but to a group of eleven young community policing agents (known as *agentes* in Portuguese), and their mid-aged female coordinator, Dona Sara. They were the remnants of a patrol group that was recruited by a community policing council that was formed by the neighbourhood administrator (*secretário do barrio*) in 2002, but which soon ceased to be active. The agents were between 22 and 35 years old, from poor families, with few years of schooling and were unemployed or had day-labour jobs when they joined the patrols. By 2009, they operated as a micro-image of a *de facto* police force, which besides regular patrols did arrests, searches, investigations and recuperation of stolen goods. They also resolved a range of crimes and disputes, informally, covering thefts, particularly of cell phones, trade in stolen goods, fraud, physical assaults, debt disputes, domestic fights, drugs and burglaries.

On a daily basis, the agents operated from a small room within the *circulo*, where they interrogated the suspects and called in the victims or parties to a dispute to deliberate cases. The *circulo* is the name used for the administrative building of the neighbourhood, which also serves as the office of the neighbourhood administrator, the Frelimo party branch, and the sector police officer who was posted in Chasana by the nearby police station to work with the "community". Thus, the agents operated from a local government venue where people reported cases, as if it was a small police station. Inside this venue, there was an observable blurring of state and civilian policing actors and practices.

The sector police officer, Basil, relied extensively on the community policing agents when he was in Chasana about two to three times a week. It quickly became clear to me that the agents had learnt much of what they did from Basil and other police officers. Already since 2003, the chief of operations at the police station had trained them in how to do searches and use handcuffs and batons in ways that do not leave visible marks. The chief of operations had also donated handcuffs and batons to them. These actions were not part of the official community-policing programme, but actually illegal. However, they reflected how the state police usurped community policing to extend state police methods and instruments to civilian agents as part of boosting police work in the neighbourhoods. Similarly, when Basil was present in Chasana, he took charge of case handling, like questioning and paperwork, but he made the agents do all kinds of tasks for him, like arresting the suspects, collecting information, delivering notice letters, and physically handling the suspects inside the *circulo*, like putting on and taking off handcuffs. On several occasions, I also observed Basil ordering an agent to beat the suspect during interrogation, according to a routinised state police method where the suspect got a set number of strokes on the buttocks while lying face down on the floor. The agents also helped Basil to accompany suspects to the police station by foot when cases could not be concluded at the *circulo*. In short, it was visibly clear that Basil outsourced the physically hard aspects of police work to the civilian agents. When Basil was present, the agents obeyed his orders, and acted as if they were under state police command.

Despite these overlaps with the state police, most crimes were not transferred to the police station, but concluded inside the neighbourhood, and thus *outside* state legal procedures. Basil, himself a state police officer, took part in some of these informal resolutions, but other cases were concluded by the agents themselves when Basil was absent. On the latter occasions, the agents mimicked how Basil operated, including how he sat on the chair, questioned the suspects, interrogated with torture and negotiated with the victims. Like Basil, they also threatened suspects by saying to them that they would transfer the case to the police station, if they did not talk or come to an agreement with the victim. They also copied state bureaucratic procedures, by having their own, yet unofficial, case register, which had the names, ID number and details of the parties and the type of case. This register was separate from the official monthly reports that Basil gave to the police station, which only included those cases that were transferred to the station. During my time of fieldwork, the official report had an average of three cases per month, whereas the agents' register had an average of two cases per day. This difference clearly indicated the scope of informalised policing. Yet equally noticeable was the continuous use of state police techniques (i.e. torture with batons, registers, reference to transfer cases to the station, and questioning methods). These techniques were frequently combined with what neighbourhood residents and the state police alike associated with community-based resolutions, which included settling crimes with compensational justice and reconciliation of the disputing parties. When cases involved severe crimes like thefts or drugs, the agents combined these methods with corporal punishments, using the batons and the beating methods that the state police had given and taught them how to use. The following case illustrates the blurriness of actors and practices that occurred in everyday policing in Chasana. Simultaneously it illustrates how blurriness is shaped both by victims' demands for informal solutions and by the mutual dependency between both sets of policing actors.

Mobile theft case

September 9, 2009, 3 PM: Louisa comes with a case to the *circulo*, which has been dealt with by the agents a month earlier. She had her cell phone stolen on the street, and reported it to the agents, who arrested the thief. At first, the thief did not want to speak up, but after the agents beat him, he said that he sold the phone to Carlos, who the agents know well as a dealer in stolen phones. Carlos was called to the *circulo*, and after being threatened with the baton, he agreed to pay Louisa for the phone on a set date. Louisa comes today to get her money, but Carlos does not turn up. She wants the agents to act immediately, but they do not want to arrest Carlos without the help of Basil, because Carlos has strong connections to organised criminals. Pedro, one of the agents, calls Basil. When Basil comes, Pedro gives a summary of the case, and Basil acts promptly by telling Pedro to fetch the handcuffs. We all walk to Carlos' house. Basil sends Pedro in, and tells Louisa and me to stay with him a bit further from the house. I wonder why Basil, as the official police officer is not the one to approach the house. Is this because the case is dealt with informally with no warrant or case number? Is Basil afraid? As I stand wondering about this issue, we are told that Carlos is not home.

On the way back to the *circulo*, I listen to a conversation between Basil and Louisa about the case procedures. Basil says that Louisa really should open a formal criminal case, because what she is facing is a crime, but then he asks her what she really wants. She says that she just wants the money so she can buy a new phone. She agreed with the agents to let the thief go free, because Carlos agreed to pay the money, and because she believes that the thief already got a punishment when the agents beat him. She does not want the police station to get involved, because "prison does not serve any good". She worries that she will not get her money if Carlos goes to prison. Basil then says that she should open a case any way, just for the accused to know that this is serious. It would be like a threat to him, Basil says, so that he would pay. Basil adds that opening a case does not mean that the perpetrator necessarily goes to prison. She can withdraw the case if she gets her money. Basil says a bit later, with a smile, that really Carlos should get into the cell (at the station), just one night, so he can learn that the case is serious. Louisa is not happy to go to the station, but she finally agrees. She comes back around 1 PM with a notification letter, which states that Carlos should appear at the station the next day. Basil gets upset, saying that this kind of notification is for social cases, not for crimes. There should be an arrest order. Nothing further happens in the case. According to Pedro, the problem is that the case is now with the police station, so the agents cannot do more. Louisa, Pedro tells me, should have never gone to the station.

As evident in Louisa's case, the blurring of state police and civilian policing actors reflected a situation of mutual dependency, which aimed to ensure both the policing actors' personal security and their capacity to get the victims a desirable outcome. Basil felt better protected when he was with the agents, he told me, because he was the only officer in the neighbourhood, and given the resource constraints of the police force, it was difficult to get reinforcement and a police car to fetch suspects. Conversely, the agents called Basil for assistance, because state police backing can provide extra strength when dealing with difficult perpetrators, like Carlos. Noticeable here is that state backing, apart from Basil's presence, predominantly takes the form of threats to transfer the case to the police station, which as Basil suggests to Louisa, may put pressure on Carlos to pay for the phone. The intention of articulating the state is not to actually instigate a formal legal process – i.e. to follow the law – but to help enforce an informal solution. So, when I speak of extra strength it is neither purely legal nor physical, but should be understood as a kind of authoritative state backing.

Here the process through which security becomes blurred is strongly influenced by popular demands for immediate and tangible justice, which stand in contrast to legal procedures. However, the state and the law come in as resources or points of reference in realising these demands. As in Louisa's case, such popular demands typically involved monetary compensation or return of stolen goods, combined with an understanding that the beatings during the interrogations also served as a kind of immediate punishment.[3] Most of my interlocutors shared Louisa's view that "prison does not serve any good". This influenced the victims' reluctance to open an official process and indeed to go to the police station.

The preference of victims to resolve cases inside the neighbourhood afforded popular legitimacy and status to the civilian agents, and by extension Basil, but simultaneously the police station remained a powerful back up. This mutual dependency, in which the blurring of security actors and practices also work to gain legitimacy and assert power, was complicated by the fact that informal resolutions also occurred at the station. As Basil said to Louisa, going to the station did not necessarily mean an official process.

During my two months of fieldwork at the police station, an average of six out of seven cases did not end with an official court process, but were, like in

Chasana, resolved informally with a focus on enforcing compensation and with the use of unofficial registers.[4] At the station, the informal resolutions had an aura of more formality and officialdom than at the *circulo*, given that they were conducted inside an official state building by uniformed and armed officers, and with the use of typewriter and register cabinets (rather than simple pens and notebooks). The existence of cells at the station, as Basil equally suggested to Louisa, also made a difference, because the officers used them to keep suspects over several days as an effective method to pressure for an agreement to pay compensation. Inside Chasana, there was no place to keep suspects overnight, and this reduced the capacity to enforce decisions. Taken together, these aspects constituted the station as a more powerful state-space than the *circulo*, because it could be used to put extra force into reaching informal resolutions.

Police state officers, like the civilian agents, equally gained popular legitimacy and could assert power by resolving cases informally (Kyed 2017b). This added a layer of competition to the collaboration between police and the civilian agents. The civilian agents had the advantage that litigants always tried to avoid the station because there was always the risk that an official process could be opened once their case was there. While this situation gave the civilian agents considerable local status and power vis-à-vis the state police, it was simultaneously through the agents' reliance on the state – as a threat and set of techniques – that they were able to resolve cases and thus gain status. State police officers faced a similar dilemma, despite their *de jure* authority. Consequently, security blurs did not only reflect collaboration, but also gave way to competitive efforts to assert police power and status, as I address next.

Boundary-making: competition, hierarchies and distinctions

As evident in the above, low-ranking state police officers depended on civilian agents and on operating *outside* the law to do their job and to assert *de facto* police authority in Chasana. This created a dilemma, because such reliance simultaneously challenged the *de jure* superior status of the police as a superior state institution. Police officers dealt with this dilemma by trying to confine their civilian agents to the informal realms of policing, through situation specific enactments of a hierarchical boundary between the state police and the agents. This was particularly noticeable when the agents acted too autonomously and when they tried to get recognition and protection within the formal realms of policing. I want to first illustrate this with field note extracts from a ceremony held in December 2009 in Chasana where a businessman gave the agents a police-like uniform.

Police uniform ceremony

Like on days of national celebration, the *circulo* is neatly organised with rows of chairs and a red tablecloth and flowers on the main office desk. It is a big day for the agents, because a young businessman has decided to donate a full uniform and instruments to them. There are ten uniforms, including trousers, shirts, belts, boots, caps, batons, handcuffs, and torches lying on the table. The local leaders, elders and the key ruling party cadres get seated. Soon after a police car pulls up. The Station Commander, Dona Laura and two officers get out of the car in full uniform and greet the others. The agents and Dona Sara are still busy in their little room, resolving a theft case, but they are now called in and told to sit at the back. The neighbourhood administrator welcomes the guests and speaks about all the hard work of the community police. He then asks Orlando, one of the agents, to put on the uniform. Orlando is displayed next to the table. He looks like a real police officer, except that the uniform is beige, rather than the usual grey and green colours of the state police uniform. Everyone claps and photos are taken. The Station Commander and the businessman pose next to Orlando (Figure 5.1).

Someone in the audience says that the uniform looks nicer than the state police's, and people laugh cautiously, as if they are unsure if the Station Commander approves. After the photo shootings, the Commander speaks to the agents: "you must work with the police and the community. You should not beat in public. This is not good. You should instead bring the persons to the *circulo* and then to the police station". She then promises the agents: "I will come by on Thursday to show you how to use the baton and the handcuffs. Otherwise you may end in prison [if you don't use them correctly]".

The donor gives the last speech, saying that he thinks the agents should be recognised for their good work and to carry a uniform that distinguishes them as police in the neighbourhood. Cheap champagne is now served to everyone, followed by lunch. The agents go to their own room, except Dona Sara, to continue hearing the theft case.

As everyone is leaving, Dona Sara assures the commander that if ever there is anything the Station needs she can contact the agents. The Commander nods and then calls the agents. She shouts: "what is this case about?" They explain and then she speaks with the victims. She then orders her officers to bring the thief to the police car. They drag him and push him harshly under the seat at the back of the pick-up police car. I am thinking that this is a good example of state and community police collaboration. At the same time, the whole act is like a police show off, as if the commander wants to demonstrate state police power by suddenly taking over the case and forcefully pushing the suspect into the car. The commander says to me: "this is how the police should work effectively".

Over the next days, I was surprised to see that the agents did not wear the new uniform. The Station Commander had called Dona Sara, telling her to wait for approval from the ministry. This approval never came. The higher echelons of the police would not allow the agents to appear like the police. They had to remain civilian. Even though the uniform was different, it still distinguished the agents as a police force, with official-like attire. The commander herself was not against the agents wearing a uniform, but she firmly supported that they should work *for* the police. They could not appear equal to or be allowed to act autonomously from the state police. The power demonstration after the ceremony was a ritualised display of this sovereign claim. It marked a hierarchical boundary between state police and civilian agents.

Figure 5.1 Show of new uniform for the community police members
Source: Photo by Helene Kyed.
Note: From the left: Police commander, businessman donor and community police agent.

Simultaneously, the commander endorsed the use of force by the agents, as evident during the ceremony, and she thus contradicted a core aspect of state sovereignty, namely the monopoly on legitimate use of violence. However, she only permitted the agents to beat as long as it remained un-displayed in public and under police supervision – otherwise the agents could get into prison, as the commander warned during the ceremony. Outside the informal realm of policing, the agents were not useful to the police, and they could not get police protection and recognition. This aspect of boundary-making was particularly evident when the agents got drawn into the more violent and extractive forms of illegal state policing. Apart from the outsourcing of torture inside the *circulo*, officers from the station and the central command of the city regularly enrolled the agents to do armed patrols and underground investigations of larger burglaries and drug trading. This was off course, entirely off the record. It also involved several operations outside Chasana. In exchange for these "services", the agents received unrecorded "salaries", likely taken from money that the police officers extracted from alleged criminals to avoid opening a formal process. The state police clearly used these forms of outsourcing to boost their power to act on serious crimes and to earn extra incomes within the illegal realms of policing. These were indeed practices that blurred security, but they could simultaneously never afford official recognition to the agents, but set them apart from the police.

While involvement in the dangerous and illegal police operations made the agents feel strong and worthy, as policing actors, they could also get them into trouble, because the agents were easier targets of complaints and threats from the criminals. With no official status and protection by the law, the agents could not defend themselves, legally, with reference to self-defence and legitimate use of force against difficult suspects, as the state police could. On a number of occasions, when bribes were taken or excessive force was used, the agents were the ones who were blamed or faced threats. For instance in a drug case, the agent Pedro gave information to a police officer, who then arrested the drug dealer, but instead of opening a case, the officer took a bribe from the dealer. A couple of days later, the dealer came to threaten Pedro with beatings if he would give information to the police again. The agents were also sometimes subject to complaints by those people who had been tortured during interrogations at the *circulo*, even when ordered by Basil. On those occasions, the police officers did try to negotiate informally with the complainants not to open a formal process, but to accept an apology or compensation. However, when one complainant, the mother of a young boy who was tortured, insisted on a formal process that ended in the district court, the police would not protect the agent. The other agents were furious and believed that the woman had bribed a police officer to open the process. Although the agent was able to raise money to pay a fine, rather serve three months in prison, the case underlined that the position of the agents remained confined to the informal realm of policing. When they trespassed the boundary of this realm, a realm that otherwise blurred state and civilian policing, they were set hierarchically apart from the state police.

The agents themselves were disillusioned with their precarious position and were displeased not to wear the new uniform. What they really wanted, they told me, was security through official recognition and remuneration from the state. Most of them wanted to become state police officers, but these dreams never materialised. They knew that they could not enter the police academy the formal way, because this requires ten years of schooling, which few of them had. However, the agent Orlando thought that the Ministry should allow the agents to enter the police college anyway, because of their field experience and hard work. Orlando submitted applications to enter the police college twice, but never got a reply. He was convinced that the authorities deliberately lost the applications. The agents strove for formal positions, but the state police needed their assistance within the informal realm of policing where benefits and powers could be reaped, but without the agents challenging the state police's claim to sovereign power.

These matters were also reflected at the national level. Although the Frelimo government endorsed the community-policing programme in 2005, no law was ever passed to recognise the community policing councils, which reached a total of 2,710 across the country in 2008. In 2010, the responsible person within the Ministry of Interior was eager to have such a law, because, as he told me, the civilian community police help to "deal with 70 percent of the crimes".[5] When I met him in 2012, he had changed his mind: there could be no law, he told me, because "community bodies should stick to community issues".[6] The problem was that many of the groups, like the agents in Chasana, had come to resemble the state police too much, he told me. Simultaneously, a city level "Council of Community Security", comprising civilian members, had become a strong voice in Maputo, which rather than simply working for the police, also wanted to report state police abuses of power and corruption. Civilian policing actors had become an alternative vector of power *outside* the regulation of the police, which challenged the *de jure* superior authority of the police, and by extension state sovereignty. This made any formal recognition a challenge to the state police, high as well as low.

Now in everyday neighbourhood policing, sovereign power was continuously contested and divided, putting into question the *de jure* position of the police, and more deeply the state. One powerful image of this was when the agents, acting autonomously, physically punished suspects, who they *outside* the law deemed perpetrators. This also frequently happened in cases where the suspects were actually transferred to the police station. While the use of force was a mimic of state-policing practices, of becoming like a police, it simultaneously positioned the agents as informal sovereigns (Hansen and Stepputat 2005) who take the law, and the baton, into their own hands, while also protecting their own precarious position vis-à-vis the police and the criminals.

Conclusion

Everyday policing in the urban neighbourhood of Chasana conveys a blurring of state and civilian security actors and practices, but this blurriness does
not evaporate efforts to assert power and enact hierarchies. Instead, what
I have tried to illustrate in this chapter is that security blurs in Chasana is
deeply conditioned by a situation of disputed sovereignty where the power to
punish and establish order is not pre-given. In this situation, we not only find
a discrepancy between state law and popular justice preferences, as scholars
of legal pluralism have argued, but also that official law enforcers – i.e. the
police – are compelled to operate through civilian agents and *outside* the law
to overcome the very limits of state sovereignty. One repercussion of this
situation is that security blurs in Chasana occur in the informalised realms
of policing, where state techniques and artefacts (investigations, torture, case
registers, notification letters, handcuffs, batons, etc., and threats of opening
a court process) become significant resources in informal solutions of crimes.

What are the deeper meanings and repercussions of this particular configuration of security blurs? As shown in this chapter, informalised policing
has both a benevolent and a violent side, concerned simultaneously with
the policing actors' efforts to gain popular legitimacy, protect themselves
and assert positions of power. On the one hand, informalised policing constitutes a response to poor urban citizens' demands for immediate justice,
like quick agreements on compensation or a swift punishment of the perpetrator. Such demands are informed by deeper urban uncertainties, not only
in terms of fear of crime, but also in the sense of livelihood insecurity, lack
of private insurance to for instance cover for property theft, and a deep dis-
trust in the law and the official legal system to protect poor urban citizens.
While the democratic transition has created awareness of citizen rights,
it has also come with increased inequalities, unemployment, rise in crime
and corruption. The urban poor feel marginalised vis-à-vis the elites who
can pay for protection and juridical processes. Because *de jure* rights have
not translated into actual protection and benefits, the poor experience the
law as unjust. Most police officers in Mozambique, and certainly the civilian policing agents, live under similar uncertain conditions, and thus share
these popular sentiments. This partly drives each set of policing actors to
resolve cases *outside* state legal procedures. Yet at stake here is also an
aspiration to gain popular legitimacy, which state police officers cannot
achieve by acting according to the law alone and without the assistance
of civilian agents, because capacities are low and their *de jure* authority,
embedded in the law, is always already disputed. Conversely, the civilian
agents depend on state police techniques and back-up to enforce informal
resolutions, which are equally important components of their capacity to
gain legitimacy and status in the neighbourhood. This mutual dependency
leads to collaboration, but also becomes a point of contestation over power
between the civilian and state policing actors.

Deeply dependent and feeding on each other, the two sets of policing actors remain in a tense relationship, especially when the civilian agents use force and decide crimes autonomously and when they try to enter the realm of formal policing and recognition – like wearing a police-like uniform, applying for Police College and asking for protection in official court cases. The dream of the civilian agents to be formally recognised is unachievable as long as the state police's *de facto* power and access to benefits rely on the informal realm of policing.

The contested relationship between civilian and state policing actors, on the other hand produces a violent side to informalised security blurs. As argued elsewhere (Kyed 2017a), a flipside of contested sovereignty is the prevalence of violence not only as a founding element of state law and authority, as Walter Benjamin (1978) argues, but also as routinised aspects of everyday policing within informal realms and through outsourcing to civilians. At a deeper level of analysis, this leads to a substitution of formal legal procedures with a more direct and naked performance of sovereign power, exemplified by the use of force as immediate punishment, investigation technique and demonstration of power. In these situations, policing takes on a law-making capacity, producing order and punishing breaches *beside* the law, and as a *substitution* for a legal process. According to Benjamin (1978, 287) the power of the police to "make law" "marks the point at which the state, whether from impotence or because of the immanent connections within any legal system, can no longer guarantee through the legal system the empirical ends that it desires at any price to attain", i.e. to assert sovereign power. A similar situation was observed with the police in Chasana. However, in that context the violence and law-making power of policing is shared, contested and equally taken up by civilian actors as an element of enacting and carving out partly autonomous spheres of power in the crime-ridden urban neighbourhoods. Moreover, these practices are not alone driven by efforts to preserve or remake state sovereignty but are also mediated by popular justice preferences. Security blurs here become the entanglement of and tensions between law, popular justice, violence and contested forms of state re-making, which reflect not simply a situation of legal pluralism, but a deeper uncertainty of sovereignty and order. The police and in particular the civilian agents, embody this uncertainty, even if blurred security simultaneously feeds and empowers them.

This takes place against the backdrop of a long history where the legitimacy of state law and the claim to a monopoly on force and social ordering have always remained pluralised and disputed (Kyed 2017a). The current democratisation process in Mozambique, which has put legal restrictions on the use of state violence – like torture during interrogations and physical punishments – further complicates the picture. The legal restrictions have increasingly situated violent performances in the less public and informalised domains. This informs the outsourcing of beatings to civilian agents by the police, but also turns violence into a means to deal with uncertainty and lack of legal protection by these civilian agents.

Notes

1 I did ethnographic fieldwork in Chasana in 2009–2010, and during 2010, I did two months fieldwork inside the police station. I did shorter follow-up fieldworks in 2011 and 2012, and re-visited in 2014, 2015 and 2016. I have changed the original name of the neighbourhood to ensure anonymisation.
2 For a detailed description of the community policing programme, see Kyed (2017c).
3 For a detailed discussion of the meanings of the physical violence applied by the civilian agents in Chasana, see Kyed (2017a).
4 In Kyed (2017b) I discuss the details of how officers inside the station dealt with social disputes and crimes by applying a mixture of state bureaucratic procedures, mediation and references to family values and traditional customs.
5 Interview, MINT responsible person for community policing, May 19, 2010.
6 Interview, MINT responsible person for community policing, November 5, 2012.

References

Abrahamsen, Rita, and Michael C. Williams. 2009. "Security Beyond the State: Global Security Assemblages in International Politics". *International Political Sociology* 3 (1): 1–17.

Araújo, Sara. 2009. "Legal Pluralism and Interlegality: The Role of Community Justices in Mozambique". In *Search of Justice and Peace: Traditional and Informal Justice Systems in Africa*, edited by Manfred Hinz and Clever Mapaure, 309–324. Berlin: Verlag.

Baker, Bruce. 2002. *Taking the Law into their Own Hands: Lawless Law Enforcers in Africa*. Burlington and Hampshire: Ashgate.

Benjamin, Walter. 1978 [1922]. "Critique of Violence". In *Reflections, Essays, Aphorisms, Autobiographical Writings*, edited by P. Demetz, 277–300. New York: Schocken.

Bertelsen, Bjørn Enge. 2016. *Violent Becomings: State Formation, Sociality and Power in Mozambique*. New York and Oxford: Berghahn Books.

Brogden, Mike, and Peetri Nijhar. 2005. *Community Policing: National and International Models and Approaches*. Devon: Willan Publishing.

Comaroff, Jean L., and John Comaroff, eds. 2006. *Law and Disorder in the Postcolony*. Chicago and London: University of Chicago Press.

Gazit, Nir. 2009. "Social Agency, Spatial Practices, and Power: the Micro Foundations of Fragmented Sovereignty in the Occupied Territories". *International Journal of Politics, Culture, and Society* 22 (1): 83–103.

Griffiths, John. 1986. "What Is Legal Pluralism?" *Journal of Legal Pluralism* 24: 1–50.

Hansen, Thomas B., and Finn Stepputat. 2001. *States of Imagination Ethnographic Explorations of the Postcolonial State*. Durham and London: Duke University Press.

Hansen, Thomas B., and Finn Stepputat, eds. 2005. *Sovereign Bodies: Citizens, Migrants and States in the Postcolonial World*. Princeton and Oxford: Princeton University Press.

Kyed, Helene M. 2007. *State Recognition of Traditional Authority. Authority, Citizenship and State Formation in Rural Post-War Mozambique.* PhD Dissertation, Roskilde University.

Kyed, Helene M. 2017a. "Predicament. Interpreting Police Violence (Mozambique)". In *Writing the World of Policing*, edited by D. Fassin, 113–138. Chicago: Chicago University Press.

Kyed, Helene M. 2017b. "Inside the Police Stations in Maputo City: Between Legality and Legitimacy". In *Police in Africa: The Street Level View*, edited by J. Beek, M. Güpfert, O. Owen, and J. Steinberg, 213–230. London: C. Hurst and Co.

Kyed, Helene M. 2017c. "Post-War Police Reform in Mozambique. The Case of Community Policing". In *Colonial Policing and Transnational Legacy: The Global Dynamics of Policing Across the Lusophone Community*, edited by C. O'Reilly, 163–182. New York: Routledge.

Kyed, Helene M. 2017d. "Hybridity and Boundary-Making: Exploring the Politics of Hybridisation". *Third World Thematics*, 2 (4): 464–480.

Kyed, Helene M., and Peter Albrecht. 2015. "Introduction: Policing and the Politics of Order-making in Urban Margins". In *Policing and the Politics of Order-Making*, edited by P. Albrecht and H.M. Kyed. New York: Routledge.

Kyed, Helene M., João Paulo Borges Coelho, Amelia Neves de Souto, and Sara Araújo, eds. 2012. *The Dynamics of Legal Pluralism in Mozambique.* Maputo: Kapicua.

Meneses, Paula. 2004. "Toward Interlegality? Traditional Healers and the Law in Postcolonial Mozambique". *Beyond Law* 30: 1–39.

Merry, Sally Engel. 1988. "Legal Pluralism". *Law and Society Review* 22 (5): 869–896.

Ministry of Interior (MINT). 2005. "Políciamento comunitário. Segurança e ordem pública, seminário nacional dos administradores distritais". October 2005.

Santos, Boaventura Souso. 2006. "The Heterogeneous State and Legal Pluralism in Mozambique". *Law and Society Review* 40 (1): 39–75.

Serra, Carlos, ed. 2008. *Linchamento em Moçambique I (Uma desordem que apela à ordem).* Maputo: Imprensa Universitária.

Tamanaha, Brian Z. 2008. "Understanding Legal Pluralism. Past to Present, Local to Global". *Sydney Law Review* 30: 375–411.

Trindade, Joao Carlos, and Boaventura de Souso Santos. 2003. *Conflito e Transformação Social. Uma Paisagem das Justiças em Moçambique.* Porto: Reino e Neves. Santa Maria da Feira.

Wood, Jennifer, and Clifford Shearing. 2007. *Imagining Security.* Devon: Willan Publishing.

6   The blurred (in)security of community policing in Bolivia

Line Jakobsen and Lars Buur

Introduction

The global security transformations that have been referred to variously as the privatisation (Abrahamsen and Williams 2011), denationalisation (Sassen 2008) and pluralisation (Loader 2000) of security enforcement is a topic that is receiving greater attention. The growing literature on the pluralisation of security enforcement provides us with numerous examples of radical cases of mobs and groups of people taking the law into their own hands and using violent means to punish those they see as offenders (Pratten and Sen 2007; Buur 2008; Diphoorn 2016), as well as the increased use of private security companies by states, firms and private individuals (Higate and Utas 2017; Abrahamsen and Williams 2011; Hönke and Müller 2012).

In the plurinational state of Bolivia, vigilante lynch violence is not uncommon. In some places, such as the cities of El Alto and Cochabamba, it is quite visible to the observer due to the "hanging dolls" from the lampposts signalling an "organized neighbourhood who lynches thieves" (Goldstein 2012; Risør 2010). In Bolivia, lynch violence is seen as emerging due to the absence of the state and by implication as an expression of the state's neo-liberalisation working under the label of "community justice"[1] (Derpic 2013; Goldstein 2012). These "extreme" versions of vigilante behaviour have attracted a great deal of scholarly attention across the world. In this chapter, we argue that the focus on these extreme forms risks overshadows subtler and more "ordinary" everyday forms of local security management. The interest here then is to look at what happens when official ideas such as community policing based on blueprints of non-violence become entangled with "informal" order-making in everyday life in places of precarious state presence. Order-making in the suburban district of Cotahuma in La Paz is not as visible or as deadly as the lynch violence that occurs in the neighbouring city of El Alto (Derpic 2013), but it shows how security is managed in and through community policing as a formal way of managing the relationship between the state and its citizens. What we will demonstrate in this chapter is how security blurs look like and are produced in the suburban area of La Paz, Bolivia, and furthermore how security is not only blurred, but how these "security blurs" also create insecurity, what we will call "blurred (in)security". When well-meaning and normally law-abiding *barrio* residents organised in neighbourhood councils are trying to work within the scheme of community policing, they at the same time slowly begin to occupy a space for action provided by the formal community policing model to exercise vigilante-like justice enforcement. Using the term (in) security here is to underline the subjective and self-identified character of "security" and not least the productivity of the processual acts of "making security" in the interface between official and unofficial ideas and practices.

As a global blueprint for action in contemporary security governance working through the community (Rose 2000; Delanty 2010), we argue that the formal and official model of community policing has, in practice, become entangled with local informal vigilante-like practices of order-making. The chapter addresses the implications of the translation of a global security technology into a local setting and looks at how "order-making" takes place and security becomes blurred in this process of implementation. The community-policing model, as conceived by the British and Bolivian authorities sponsoring and implementing its transfer, builds on the inclusion of the community as an active player in the provision of security, but coordinated and controlled by the official community-policing officers. In this process of the blurring of security, boundaries are constantly negotiated in the way individuals and groups position themselves as belonging to certain moral categories and communities and detaching themselves from others. As both *barrio* residents and policemen work with the community-policing model at the boundary of the state,[2] they are reconfiguring claims of sovereignty in the process. The manifestations of security we have identified are, in practice, made up by a myriad set of actors and perceptions of what is really secure. We argue that, in the process of implementing the official community-policing model in order to make everyday life on the hillsides of La Paz safer, a type of security blur is produced, and what we will show in this chapter is that a new type of insecurity is co-produced in this "making of security".

This chapter is the elaboration and culmination of research conducted by Line Jakobsen for her Master's thesis during lengthy stays in La Paz, Bolivia, between 2013 and 2014. The first period of fieldwork was carried out in late 2013, the second and longer period between August and December 2014. In combining Line's findings with Buur's earlier work on community policing in South Africa, new perspectives appeared, which have resulted in this book chapter.

In the following section, we will describe how security and insecurity are experienced in the urban periphery of La Paz. Based on this we will give examples of the everyday encounters through which new ontological understandings and enactments of security develop, showing how the formal community-policing model becomes entangled with local security practices.

The context of insecurity

The *barrios*[3] of Llojeta, Tembladerani and Higher and Lower Pasankeri all belong to the macro-district of Cotahuma on the hillsides bordering the cities of La Paz and El Alto. Lower middle class families inhabit the district, which, according to the authors' own calculations, contain approximately 50,000–60,000 inhabitants. As one resident explained, the *barrios* are located where "the asphalt" at the outer edge of the city of La Paz stops and the dirt roads begin. To live on the edge of the city where the asphalt stops is a common way of characterising the experience residents have of living on the margins of the state. "State margins" (Das and Poole 2004) are understood here as being "situated in the very bodies of people". In spite of the fact that in spatial terms the state, physically reflected in the government's palace and the central police station, are located within five kilometres, and state law does inform life on the hillsides, Cotahuma's residents do not feel included in the community of the state. Indeed, they constantly experience what they call "incompliances" from the state. In these *barrios*, there is a fear of what Buur (2006, 2008) has elsewhere referred to as a "polyvalent concept of crime" that is omnipresent yet hard to pin down for *barrio* residents, as it can take many different forms such as criminal offences like killings, robberies, break ins, to forms of communal disorder like unruly behaviour, indiscipline, moral transgressions.

The uncertainty of not knowing precisely what, where and who could be dangerous informs everyday life in these *barrios*. The polyvalent concept of crime described in interviews included robberies, alcoholism, public and domestic violence, the consumption and sale of drugs, corruption, bad management of garbage and traffic problems, prostitution and human trafficking (see also Observatorio Nacional de Seguridad Ciudadana 2013; LAPOP 2014). The accounts of *barrio* residents tend to be mixed up and unified in what residents repeated several times during fieldwork: "There is a lot of the '*anti-social*'". In speaking this way, the *anti-social*, which normally refers to the behaviour or features of a person, is turned into a phenomenon of excess; some*thing* there "is a lot of". The dangers of "the anti-social" and others whom are seen as working against "the social" or the community, could be practically any*body*. "The anti-social" seems to cover robbery, rape, gangs, alcoholism, prostitution, corrupt policemen, new neighbours not following the norms of the *barrio* etc. (Notes from fieldwork, November 2014).

This way of conceptualising "danger" is not held by the residents of the *barrios* alone, but is also an idea shared with the police. According to the *Policía Boliviana* (PB 2009), "the threats are constant [. . .] we never know the capacity of the persons until the day they hurt us [. . .] the enemy never sleeps, and we always have it closer to us than we imagine". This was how the police argued in a key document used in community-policing training, which exemplifies the inherent ambivalence regarding who "the enemy" is. As it is not a permanent feature of any*body*, one day even the policeman could be deemed an "enemy" of the community. This uncertainty for both policemen and residents is something we will return to in the following sections.

In order to manage the insecurity, during 2014 the La Paz municipality ran huge campaigns addressing citizen security where "community police" had been mentioned repeatedly as "the new thing" that could be the solution to the problem of crime. The official model of community policing was transferred to Bolivia from the United Kingdom in 2005, based on British funding and expertise. After a slow start, community policing became part of the idea of "citizen security" that has emerged throughout Latin America as an alternative to repressive state security and the infamous *Mano Dura* (iron fist) policies (Goldstein et al. 2007). The notion of "citizen security" involves a special focus on policing for citizens and an acknowledgement of the importance of the community participating in security provision.

The role of "the community" in community policing

The idea of the community-policing model in Bolivia was to build on civic groups that had already been officially established by the Law on Popular Participation of 1994. These are the Neighbourhood Councils,[4] the School Brigades for Security and the Civil Support Groups to the Police (PB 2014b, 94). These pre-existing neighbourhood formations were supposed to be strengthened through and co-opted within the community-policing system. The new component, which came with community policing, is the promotion of "Neighbourhood Security Brigades", community-based organisations led by the Bolivian police whose task is to create a culture of public security and "peaceful coexistence of communities" (PB 2014a, 2014b) by working through a block system to capture all the households in their areas (PB 2014b, 115–117).

The particular discourse related to "community", we suggest, is based on changing values and behaviour as a mechanism of inclusion into the "right community" of the state, a community in which citizenship becomes a value, something that one can earn through good behaviour. In practicing this, political subject positions come into being, as *barrio* residents claim the right to security and are recognised as subjects with "the right to have rights" whereby they become citizens (Schramm and Krause 2011, 117 inspired by Hannah Arendt). The police strongly emphasise that the community, as a "client", is a co-producer of security: residents should participate actively in the creation of a "culture of security" and educate their children to become virtuous citizens. In order to achieve this, "ordinary people" are retrained so they are ready to play an active part in the promotion of a "culture of security" and as such, be direct assistants of the police, in line with the philosophy of community policing and the state logic of law and order.

Invitation to participate

The creation of a "culture of security" is based on one's private responsibility to be a good citizen and create a safe atmosphere. Various police documents stress that, for community policing to succeed in creating security, a shift in mentality and behaviour is needed by both the police and residents

(PB 2014b). Based on mantras such as "without the people, there is no police" (workshop notes, October 21, 2014) and "the neighbour knows the people living in his (or her) street best", the police try to mobilise *barrio* residents. Local knowledge is the key to understanding who the proper residents of the *barrio* are and knowing "whether they work or not, if they are involved in any suspect activities" (EPB 2013, 60). This, we suggest, is a key example of neo-liberal processes of the responsibilisation of public security, where tasks that were formerly conceived as belonging to the state (Rose 2000, 324; Deukmedjian 2013, 66; Garland 2002, 124) are now delegated from the state to the communities. By codifying and delimiting the exercise of social control through laws and the use of the community-policing model, the Bolivian state aims to recapture its control and legitimacy by formally pursuing a process of decentralising state control that at the same time is an attempt to recentralise control over specific populations. This type of governance implies a transformation from trying to regulate everything through the centralisation of power to regulation by means of indirect government through the self-interest of the community (Deukmedjian 2013).

While the invitation to form a partnership with the police was formally communicated and implemented, it nonetheless became clear during fieldwork among both residents of the district of Cotahuma and La Paz police officers in charge of implementing the policing model that it had largely failed. The police had not succeeded in constructing a police force of "communitarian cops" as intended, nor in making "the community" ready to participate in accordance with the state logic of security. As is also argued elsewhere (Brenner et al. 2010) "reform failures" can nonetheless be highly productive. Orienting the lens towards the productivity of "failures" or, to put it in other words, unexpected effects, of implementations of official ideas is one of the central tasks of social research we argue. In our case, *barrio* residents were fully aware of how they could use the new space for active participation that they were given through the (failed) implementation of the state's new citizen security model of 2004 (community policing). This happened, as we will see, as *barrio* residents came to use the logic of the model's vague component of citizen responsibilisation productively to deal with the *anti-social* in ways that were not expected by the state. This is what we focus on in the following section.

The emergence of blurred (in)security

How have formal ideas of community policing become entangled with informal vigilante practices and in that process producing security blurs, which is also producing insecurity or, as we will call it here, "blurred (in) security"? In order to answer this, we will briefly present some testimonies of *barrio* residents' experiences with the police, as this is their way of creating meaning for their own version of community policing and vigilante-like activities.

Despite the general interest among *barrio* residents in having a more democratic, transparent, efficient and well-functioning police force and "more police officers on the ground" (interview with Marcos, 24/1/14), the attitude towards the police is rather negative among *barrio* residents. Local security experts and observers we interviewed from the Bolivian Observatory for Peace and Security echoed this, and they suggested that, in order to reform the police as an institution, the police should be closed down and rebuilt from scratch. Descriptions of the ordinary policeman given by both police leaders and community members generally involve adjectives such as "lazy", "disloyal" and "corrupt". One *barrio* resident expressed his despair about police behaviour, referring to them as failing in their paternal role of the "sovereign": "In a way I see you [the police] as the parents of the neighbours, but despite this [. . .] the police are the first to break the law in all cases" (resident, Community Policing workshop, October 21, 2014).

Residents explained how the police cooperate with so-called "trick thieves" and commit minor violations of the law of all kinds every day. As the policeman is "he who manages and orders [. . .] the maximum authority" (resident, workshop 21/10/14), "it is difficult to teach them" the complaint went. According to *barrio* residents, the police officers are as unreliable as the criminals, as:

> You do not know whether they [the police] will attend the case", whether "they will ignore it" or whether "they will turn out to be the offender" or "will assault you [even] worse [than the criminal]" or "if he is going to rape you".[5]
>
> (Interviews with four residents,
> October and November 2014)

This experience of the police as those you cannot rely on means, according to *barrio* residents, that there is no confidence in the police as an institution and therefore "there is no coordination" between the community and the police. According to Carmen, a *barrio* resident speaking on behalf of her neighbours, it is the police themselves who create the insecurity:

> Before – I am talking about twenty years ago – the *barrio* was a very quiet area. You didn't hear about robberies, you didn't hear about assaults. Sadly and unfortunately [. . .] the police came, and the attacks on houses began.

What Carmen suggests is that insecurity came with the establishment of the local community police station, illustrating the inherent ambivalence *barrio* residents have towards the police. Here those who represent what a resident called "the maximum authority" (the police as a stand-in for the state), which ideally should protect its citizens, are also those who produce (in) security blurs, as the very attempt to create security in itself produces a deep perception of insecurity. This ambivalent attitude to the police comes close to Dennis Rodgers' (2006) depiction of "the State as a Gang" or Beatrice Jauregui's (2015, 41) analysis of "police vigilantism" as "a mode of authoritative extra-legal coercion performed by public police officials conceived as doing their duty to realise justice in the world". Sovereignty is here a result or product of "performance" (Hansen and Stepputat 2006), which often means that the sovereign position of the police is inherently ambivalent in its constitution, drawing on both profane (failure) and sublime (ideal expectations) elements (Hansen 2001).

This ambivalent understanding of the police has consequences when the community-policing model is translated into a Bolivian context. When the police approach *barrio* residents to educate them about community policing, in a process where *barrio* residents both acknowledge the sovereignty of the state and simultaneously conform the existence of "the community" for the police, what is it that residents hear? They first of all hear that they are the key actors, being invited and encouraged to be active participants by the police. However, in a group interview with four residents, it was expressed how this formal invitation from the police to participate in community policing is interpreted slightly differently from what was intended by the policing model:

JUAN: "Now, look, I tell you, and this is true, what do the police say? 'Organize yourself!'" [. . .]

ROSELYN: "There are people who want to take justice into their own hands because there is no trust in the police. There is none now".

JUAN: "We have been in many seminars where the police have told us very clearly to organize ourselves". [. . .]

ROSELYN: "What does that tell you? 'Organize as neighbours', that's like, 'make your own justice, because the police can't'".

(Group interview, 29/10/14)

In these interview extracts, we suggest, the community policing model is interpreted as a call both to organise and for the community to take the law into its own hands. This, we propose, blurs the lines between public and private, formal and informal, civil and uncivil, legal and illegal, productive for understanding how blurred (in)security enforcement becomes the norm. Following Sharma and Gupta (2006, 16), the line between "the state" and the "non-state realms" is partly drawn by the everyday mundane work of bureaucrats and their encounters with those they should serve. What happens when *barrio* residents slowly become "bureaucrats"? In the next section, we suggest the line between the police and vigilante activities becomes entangled and blurred in practice.

When "ordinary people" become "police officers"

The experience of the police as those you cannot count on is important when understanding how community policing, in its entanglement with local security practices, produces blurred (in)security. As coordination between the police and the community is lacking, the *barrio* residents more often refer to *barrio* presidents or neighbourhood councils as the *de facto* authorities who are in a better position to safeguard local order than the official police. One *barrio* president explains how he spends almost half of his working hours during the week on "community affairs", solving problems for his neighbours related to perceived acts of the *anti-social* (interview with Gonzalo, January 2014). When we visited Marcos, the Head of the Committee for Social Control, in his home, people often came by to have him solve a problem related to the *anti-social*, at the same time expecting him to be able to claim rights or funds that they cannot access. Besides this, the councillors normally visited neighbours who were causing trouble in order to educate or discipline them. Often the problems were about raising awareness of problems with alcoholism, drugs and prostitution, especially among the youth.

Besides the everyday order-making, local residents also regularly go on patrol when needed. According to three residents of Tembladerani, mounting civil patrols is the only alternative, now that police control "makes no sense":

JUAN: "I tell you, [civil patrolling is] the only alternative, the only alternative here, because if we wait for police help, we wait in vain, being very honest".

ROSELYN: "I also think so, because they run from the control. Due to a lack of resources, we know that. [. . .] But it does not give the right, nor the place for the citizens to endure so much violence".

(Group interview, 29/10/14)

The logic is that, as the police do not do their job, the *barrio* residents themselves have to enforce order. This is a common attitude among community members. What is also interesting is that Roselyn uses the word "right" (*derecho*); the lack of resources available to the police "does not give the right" to "so much violence". Instead it becomes "right" that the residents take on the task of patrolling themselves. At the same time, it was clear that *barrio* residents indeed try to coordinate their crime prevention tasks with the police, rather than antagonise them from the outset.[6] As they experience being "let down", they start organising themselves and slowly move away from formal law enforcement.

An account from a community member shows how members act when they meet a "suspect" of the *anti-social*. Gonzalo, the president of the neighbourhood council in Tembladerani, talked us through their "police-like" activity:

Barely seeing someone suspicious or someone who I don't know . . . is standing for a long time, then he is approached and asked, "Let's hear, who are you looking for?" [Then] he doesn't know what to answer and suspiciously, for example, [the residents tell him] "leave before the neighbours come out".

(Gonzalo 26/1/14)

By making a veiled threat of mob violence as a punishment for "standing there and acting suspiciously", Gonzalo ensures that such strangers do not come back into his neighbourhood. The threat is also symbolised by the use of the whistle that Juan, a Tembladerani resident introduced us to. The reasoning is that, if all the neighbours blow their whistles (demonstrating the "mass" of the people with sound) when a stranger enters the neighbourhood suspected of *anti-social* behaviour, he gets the message that he has entered a well-organised community and will not come back (group interview, 29/10/14). Defining an "organised community" by whistling becomes an instrument with which to create a sense of security, just as the hanging dolls might symbolise for El Alto or Cochabamba residents when they demonstrate how they deal with the *anti-social*. A sense of security, we suggest, is based on feeling like a member of "the social" that created the community. In this sense the whistle becomes the object that connects two essential values for the *barrio* residents, namely "security" and "community".

The whistle, symbolising an active community engagement and alertness stands, according to the residents, in contrast to the slowness of the police and the lack of coordination between the police and the community. This is framed by Jorge, who explained how the police:

> Wait until you are bloody all over, with broken arms, to just then make the accusation, and even when this happens, they disengage themselves from it all, they say "no, no we don't attend this case [. . .] you already have the proof, and it is only conciliations between neighbours".
>
> (Jorge 26/1/14)

Thus, according to Jorge, the police react too slowly (not until you bleed and they have broken your arm), try to avoid their responsibilities and do not treat the "suspicions" of residents as "real" incidents they have to act upon. Instead, the local residents have already "done the work" by having captured the *anti-social* or beaten the criminal, so they can present the proof when the police arrive, resulting in the latter's "disengagement" (ibid.). In conclusion, the community – without the police – ends up becoming not only the executive arm of security enforcement, but also the judiciary, as well as the legislature – the writer of the moral law of the community, which is contrary to the *trias politica* model that underpins the neo-liberal global community-policing model.

As we described above, however, to a great extent community policing is aimed at building trust and responsibilisation among the community so that community members are motivated to work as the extended arm of the police. The policing model is based on the rationale that barrio residents organise themselves to carry out patrols and do general security work *coordinated by the police* (PB 2014b). However, the residents of Cotahuma experience another reality in their neighbourhoods. According to them, the police do not keep their promises and agreements, and can suddenly appear to be affiliated with criminal activities of various types, as already mentioned. That the police have come closer to the community (in both concrete and symbolic ways) has not created more security, but instead the contrary, as the *barrio* residents told us. Here lies the paradox of the exercise: the challenge is to make police officers and *barrio* residents follow the same mental schemes for defining the *anti-social*, its "dangers" and what "security" is. Instead, when residents take on the task of "doing security", originally thought of as belonging to the state, the line between state and non-state becomes blurred. Through its vernacularisation, community policing as a global blueprint for action hence becomes the model for blurred security, law and order, which *de facto* produces insecurity.

Blurred (in)security and boundary-drawing

State law normally operates by imposing its own perceptions and schemes of order. In this case, however, the scheme does not necessarily comply with the logic of the *barrio* residents. We agree with Goldstein (2012) when he suggests that the ambivalent positions of "law" and "illegality" in the Bolivian political landscape produce an inconsistency that blurs the boundaries of what is and is not state. When *barrio* residents try to establish security following "their" scheme of order by utilising the language and symbols of the state (Gupta 1995; Hansen and Stepputat 2006) – that is, by claiming their space and responsibility for taking part in community policing work – this is accorded legitimacy and legality, even though it might mean working on the margins of the state's law. It is interesting that, although residents may perceive the state as inefficient, they generate state-like proposals as answers to the problems they see as being created by the same state's incapacity. This stresses that we should not understand these residents as gangs or mobs of violent vigilantes. The way that the hillside residents enact different political subjectivities makes it hard to give their type of "active citizenship" a label, as it is constantly balancing on the edge of the law, sometimes working within the domain of the state and at other times outside it.

In this blurred domain, however, we also see continuous efforts to draw and negotiate boundaries between "right" and "wrong". During fieldwork, lynch violence became the schism that all practices were positioned in relation to, though without providing us with a clear-cut and coherent picture of what was "right" and "wrong". Roselyn and her fellow hillside residents stressed that the methods of their neighbours in El Alto, who use lynch violence as a way of dealing with the *anti-social* – for example, as a way of punishing intruders – is a crime and therefore itself "anti-social" behaviour that should not happen. However, the residents also state that sometimes "self-defence" (as in "doing it yourself") is the only way to manage (in)security. When asked where the limit lies for the self-management of law enforcement, they answered, "There is none now" (group interview, 29/10/14), though in this case they seemed to want to describe current practice as something that constantly crosses the limits, rather than demarcate their own normative stand on the matter.

When asked whether lynching is a crime or a solution to the problems faced by the *barrio*, Carmen and her neighbours stated that "it is a crime", but added:

CARMEN: "But maybe, at the same time, they [the 'lynchers'] liberate us from [. . .] a thief".

ROSELYN: "They are liberating us"

CARMEN: "They are liberating all of us [. . .] that is why that justice is sometimes applied [. . .] Obviously the police should take care of this [. . .] if the police are already overrun, what should be done? Just defend yourself, do it in self-defence. There is no other way. That's the problem".

(Group interview, 29/10/14)

Despite the fact that they see lynching as a crime, they accept it and stress how they might benefit from it. They also underline that there is, in practice, no firm or clear boundary between the law and lynch violence. Gonzalo, President of Pasankeri, and Jorge, President of Tembladerani, were the two local leaders who tried to draw these boundaries most clearly of all the informants, though even their definition, it turns out, is still affected by the blurriness between state law and illegality. Gonzalo tried to present this distinction between legitimate and illegitimate behaviour by referring to a workshop on citizen security he had attended. At the workshop, they were taught "how to defend ourselves, how to avoid, how should I explain this to you . . .", and after a rather long pause for thought, he continued, "Once upon a time . . . delinquents have been killed in Pasankeri" (Gonzalo 26/1/14). This they have to learn to avoid, he argued. Jorge also condemned lynch violence, stating clearly that "Here, we don't participate like that" after explaining how a lynching happens "up there" (i.e. in El Alto). Lynching had happened "before", both *barrio* presidents stated, "with the excuse that it was in self-defence" (ibid.). The method Gonzalo and his *barrio* use today, which they perceive as following the guidance of the authorities and the formal policies regarding citizen security, is described by Gonzalo as follows: "in this way, we pass around here with whistles, signals; we all come out to capture him, he is beaten up (*dan paliza*) and handed in (to the police)" (ibid.).

We believe this *modus operandi* exemplifies well the blurriness we are trying to understand. On the one hand, Gonzalo wants to signal that, as active citizens, they are now on "the right track". Whereas before they killed criminals, as they still do in El Alto, now they work with the police, or at least follow some official police procedures. On the other hand, Gonzalo and his neighbours still legislate (set the law for what is *anti-social*), judge and punish by beating up the offender, which happens before the criminal is handed over to the police, if (s)he ever is. As a group of outraged neighbours confronting danger and risks, they believe it is their right – or at least necessary – to define what is a crime and what is order before the police take over and give their judgement.

This becomes a way for community members to take control and manage uncertainty, to "discipline" the suspicious and *anti-social* and to make sure that "criminals" do not return to the *barrio*. Once the *barrio* residents have defined right and wrong in their area, it is up to the police to do the "bureaucracy", which the residents do not perceive as very efficient. We have not been able to trace any case in which the residents have been either captured by the police or condemned by the community when they have beaten up a criminal. Rather, it seems informally to become the proper management of crime in the *barrio*. This resonates with Helene Risør's (2010, 126) study of policing in El Alto, where the boundary of legitimate self-defence described by the police was drawn between beating up a criminal and lynching him. Here we see how *barrio* residents – even though they do not carry out deadly lynching, but only "casual beatings" – become those who invoke a state of exception, in which they can decide on the life of the offender as an informal expression of the sovereign[7] operating with impunity.

Even though it is common to condemn the police for their failure to solve the *anti-social*, be it community problems, delinquency or crime, self-policing with or without violence becomes tolerated and justified. As already outlined, the *barrio* residents on the hillsides of La Paz are afraid of thieves and other *anti-socials* entering their neighbourhoods. The uncertainty about the police is that "you never know whether he will help or assault you" and this co-produces the feeling of insecurity. We argue that collective fear, nurtured through the media and public discourses, as well as daily small talk within communities, helps justify violence, as it has the ability to establish a self-referential logic that can lead to a "state of exception" (Ägamben 1998, 53) involving what could be called the "vernacular securitisation" (Bubandt 2005 drawing on; Buzan et al. 1998 and their idea of securitisation) of day-to-day community life. Walking the streets of the *barrio*, meeting up in a central square, even being in your house becomes "a security matter". Quotidian securitisation appears to be a productive force for actions on the frontiers of the state, as the "usual" ethical standards are temporarily put aside.

Bubandt (2005) suggests that securitisation is a discursive device for community-building, that is, for the rhetorical evocation and political realisation of imagined communities. Built out of the fear of crime, we suggest, the communal responsibility to react to "suspicious activities" that is inherent in community policing paradoxically constructs a sense of community that both works on the edge of the state and is central to it. Concerned *barrio* residents who are willing to organise and take considerable measures to establish order and safety in their community are involved in a constant struggle over what is morally correct conduct and what is not; what is a legitimate exercise of authority and what is not (see also Buur and Jensen

2004, 145). As these boundaries are neither stable nor very clear-cut – not even for the residents of Cotahuma – "right" and "wrong" in these semi-formal community-policing practices becomes a question of what actually takes place in each individual case: it does not necessarily follow any written rules. This ambivalence is part of the blurriness through which citizens slowly become what we might call performers of sovereignty (Hansen and Stepputat 2006). However, as with the case of Cotahuma, this version of blurred security also produces insecurity, as one can never be certain of when which law (whether the formal or informal) will be applied, whether the punishment will be violent or not, and who the *"anti-social"* really is in the defence of the law.

Political subjectivities and blurred (in)security

We argue that, through community-based self-policing, as we see it on the hillsides of La Paz, the "community" is reiterated, and "active neighbours" become the new legitimate authority.[8] Buur and Jensen (2004) similarly suggest, in their article on South Africa, that "[t]he continual practices of everyday policing are what constitute the formation of the moral community, which is the basis for the production of localized sovereignty and authority" (ibid., 146). Evoking the political subjectivity of the *vecino* (Spanish for neighbour) on the hillsides of La Paz, we argue, really means being included in the community of *barrio* life in the urban periphery. The community that the residents share builds on notions of solidarity and the collective feeling of being left "without control" by the state. Based on this sense of community, they can defy their position on the "periphery" and confront the state as a "social front of neighbours" (resident, workshop, 21/10/14). According to *barrio* residents, they can only trust themselves and their neighbours. The "bad neighbours" are either excluded or motivated to change their behaviour so that it fits community norms, as "community" and "security" become mutually constitutive. The neighbours who choose to "close the curtains" (Carmen, group interview 29/10/14) instead of collaborating, fall outside of the community and instead become part of the problem, as they cannot be counted on and hence show their proximity to the *anti-social*.

Understanding these multiple claims of belonging as expressions of political subjectivities makes it possible to see how local communities can be political in many ways and how the relational dynamics through which power comes into play do not necessarily have to be linked to citizenship in a nation state (Schramm and Krause 2011). In that sense, it also helps us understand how other forms of authority seem to evolve as expressions of sovereignty. This is seen most clearly in the way residents always seem to direct their claims primarily to the local leaders of the neighbourhood or to the leader of the Committee for Social Control.

On the frontier of the state, alongside state actions, "ordinary citizens" organise to maintain law and order on behalf of their communities. As security providers, they are most often pragmatic and humble community members, working on the margins of the law out of necessity, rather than in direct opposition to it, deploying all the available resources that look like state practices and maintaining a blueprint of legitimacy. As with Chatterjee's (2004, 40) political society, at times *barrio* residents consider it necessary to cross the boundary to "live and work". Abrahams (2007, 422) calls the arena in which this takes place "an awkward borderland between law and illegality", recalling this volume's idea of security blurs. This blurriness is not only constantly produced, it is also productive, as it creates spaces for action in which the Bolivian police and local communities can perform social control and struggle to make life less insecure for themselves, their families and their neighbourhood. Paradoxically, the perceived absence of the state is at the same time what makes the state present, in line with Goldstein's (2012) idea of "the phantom state". In pragmatic ways, the hillside residents try to manage a situation in which, on the one hand, they are watched and closely embedded in both state control and social control, while on the other hand they find themselves in need of services, resources and security.

Conclusion

In this chapter, we have seen how the hillside residents classify themselves as those who do not practice lynch violence but are ready to work with the police. We have also seen how blurred security produces insecurity, or blurred (in)security, as we have called this double movement. We have focused on how blurred (in)security has been managed, as the danger of the *anti-social* seems to be everywhere. The polyvalent and uncertain character of "crime" means that *barrio* residents and police alike continually try to distinguish the criminal from the active citizen. In Bolivia the police themselves represent the blurriness of security and become part of the polyvalent character of "the danger" that produces the sense of insecurity. As the police possess the same unstable character as the criminal, their authority is questioned not only by the residents, but also by the police themselves, as the discussions related to community policing illustrate. Thus, in performing a diagnosis of current community policing, it could be argued that the policing model *de facto* reproduces its own *raison d'être*. The uncertain character of the police, the threats from the *anti-social*, as well as the informal and ad hoc order-making practices of the *barrio* residents, we suggest, are all factors that form the blurred context of (in)security on the hillsides of La Paz.

This chapter has demonstrated how community policing, through its somewhat subversive transformation in Bolivia, has created competing local security practices and plural forms of authority and expressions of sovereignty. The *barrio* residents have taken the space for action that the responsibilisation mechanisms of the community-policing model have given them, to perform their own version of community law-making and policing. As the *barrio* residents are organised into bodies defined by law and are expected to become engaged in security work through community policing, the communities take over a legitimate space in which to mobilise and conduct social control. The paradox is that community policing reproduces state sovereignty while simultaneously challenging it. In doing so, communities continually oscillate between legality and illegality according to their own interpretations of "law", "order" and "right" (much like the police do, by the way), sometimes subscribing to state law, while at other times moving beyond it. As a result, we conclude that *barrio* residents perform a subtle kind of expression of sovereignty. In this respect, global community-policing "blueprints" have become something else in practice among local communities, and ultimately community policing *de facto* produces blurred (in)security.

Notes

1 The State Constitution of 2009 (Estado Plurinacional de Bolivia 2009) acknowledges legal pluralism by law, implying that the indigenous peasant justice system can function in parallel to the ordinary justice system. In popular debates in Bolivia, "community justice" often becomes the concept covering both this indigenous justice system and vigilante lynch justice, thus confusing the two practices. It can be argued, however, that the formal acceptance of indigenous justice as a legitimate security practice works to cover for, or justify, the extra-legal and violent expressions of mob violence.
2 Or other actors such as private security companies, which cannot be discussed at length in this chapter.
3 *Barrio* is the Spanish for neighbourhood.
4 In Spanish: *juntas vecinales*.
5 Roselyn's statement about the risk of being raped also clearly exposes the gendered nature of authority. Also see Diphoorn (2015).
6 The same argument was presented by Jorge Derpic (2015) in a paper presented at the LASA2015 conference.
7 "Expression of sovereignty" has been used by Buur (2006) as a way of talking about sovereignty outside the domain of the state where vigilantes or other social groups take on and perform various acts that draw on while still challenging state sovereignty.
8 This is in line with Risør (2010), who studied "neighbourhoodness" in El Alto, but not La Paz.

References

Abrahams, David. 2007. "Some Thought on the Comparative Study of Vigilantism". In *Global Vigilantes*, 419–440. London: Hurst.

Abrahamsen, Rita, and Michael Williams. 2011. *Security Beyond the State: Private Security in International Politics*. New York: Cambridge University Press.

Agamben, Giorgio. 1998. *Homo Sacer: Sovereign Power and Bare Life*. Stanford: Stanford University Press.

Brenner, Neil, Jamie Peck, and Nik Theodore. 2010. "Variegated Neoliberalization: Geographies, Modalities, Pathways". *Global Networks* 10 (2): 182–222.

Bubandt, Nils. 2005. "Vernacular Security: The Politics of Feeling Safe in Global, National and Local Worlds". *Security Dialogue* 36 (3): 275–296.

Buur, Lars. 2006. "Reordering Society: Vigilantism and Expressions of Sovereignty in Port Elizabeth's Townships". *Development and Change* 37 (4): 735–757.

Buur, Lars. 2008. "Democracy & Its Discontents: Vigilantism, Sovereignty & Human Rights in South Africa". *Review of African Political Economy* 35 (118): 571–584.

Buur, Lars, and Steffen Jensen. 2004. "Introduction: Vigilantism and the Policing of Everyday Life in South Africa". *African Studies* 63 (2): 139–152.

Buzan, Barry, Ole Wæver, and Jaap de Wilde. 1998. *Security: A New Framework for Analysis*. Boulder: Lynne Rienner Pub.

Chatterjee, Partha. 2004. *The Politics of the Governed: Reflections on Popular Politics in Most of the World*. Leonard Hastings Schoff Memorial Lectures. New York: Columbia University Press.

Das, Veena, and Deborah Poole, eds. 2004. *Anthropology in the Margins of the State*. 1st edition. School of American Research Advanced Seminar Series. Santa Fe; Oxford: School of American Research Press; James Currey.

Delanty, Gerard. 2010. *Community. Key Ideas*. 2nd edition. London and New York: Routledge.

Derpic, Jorge. 2013. "Bolivia: Los linchados de El Alto". *Revista Anfibia, Universidad de Texas* (blog). www.revistaanfibia.com/cronica/bolivia-los-linchados-de-el-alto/.

Derpic, Jorge. 2015. "Vigilantes or Community Police. Citizens' Involvement in Crime Prevention Tasks". Paper Prepared for delivery at the 2015 Congress of the Latin American Studies Association, Puerto Rico, May 27–30, 2015.

Deukmedjian, John Edward. 2013. "Making Sense of Neoliberal Securitization in Urban Policing and Surveillance: Neoliberal Securitization in Urban Policing and Surveillance". *Canadian Review of Sociology/Revue Canadienne de Sociologie* 50 (1): 52–73.

Diphoorn, Tessa. 2015. "'It's All About the Body': The Bodily Capital of Armed Response Officers in South Africa". *Medical Anthropology* 34 (4): 336–352. https://doi.org/10.1080/01459740.2015.1027342.

Diphoorn, Tessa. 2016. *Twilight Policing: Private Security and Violence in Urban South Africa*. Berkeley: University of California Press.

EPB 2013, Perspectivas de la Seguridad Ciudadana en América Latina y Bolivia Intercambio de Buenas Prácticas, Memoria del Seminario Internacional, Santa Cruz de la Sierra, 27–28/12, Ministerio de Gobierno, Estado Plurinacional de Bolivia

Estado Plurinacional de Bolivia. 2009. "Constitución Política del Estado (CPE)". https://bolivia.infoleyes.com/norma/469/constituci%C3%B3n-pol%C3%ADtica-del-estado-cpe.

Garland, David. 2002. *The Culture of Control: Crime and Social Order in Contemporary Society*. Oxford: Oxford University Press.

Goldstein, Daniel M. 2012. *Outlawed: Between Security and Rights in a Bolivian City*. A John Hope Franklin Center Book. Durham: Duke University Press.

Goldstein, Daniel M., With Gloria Achá, Eric Hinojosa, and Theo Roncken. 2007. "La Mano Dura and the Violence of Civil Society in Bolivia". *Social Analysis* 51 (2).

Gupta, Akhil, ed. 1995. "Blurred Boundaries: The Discourse of Corruption the Culture of Politics, and the Imagined State". In *The Anthropology of the State: A Reader*, 2006: 211–243. Blackwell Readers in Anthropology 9. Malden and Oxford: Blackwell Publishing.

Hansen, Thomas Blom. 2001. "Governance and State Mythologies in Mumbai". In *States of Imagination*, edited by Thomas Blom Hansen, Finn Stepputat, George Steinmetz, and Julia Adams, 221–254. Durham: Duke University Press.

Hansen, Thomas Blom, and Finn Stepputat. 2006. "Sovereignty Revisited". *Annual Review of Anthropology* 35 (1): 295–315.

Higate, Paul R., and Mats Utas. 2017. *Private Security in Africa: From the Global Assemblage to the Everyday.* London: Zed Books.

Hönke, Jana, and Markus-Michael Müller. 2012. "Governing (in)Security in a Post-colonial World: Transnational Entanglements and the Worldliness of 'Local' Practice". Edited by Jana Hönke and Markus-Michael Müller. *Security Dialogue* 43 (5): 383–401.

Jauregui, Beatrice. 2015. "Just War: The Metaphysics of Police Vigilantism in India". *Conflict and Society* 1 (1).

LAPOP. 2014. "Cultura Política de La Democracia En Bolivia 2014: Hacia Una Democracia de Ciudadanos, Resumen Del Estudio Nacional". *Comunidad de Estudios Sociales y Acción Pública and Proyecto de Opinión Pública En América Latina and Ciudadanía Bolivia*, La Paz, Bolivia.

Loader, Ian. 2000. "Plural Policing and Democratic Governance". *Social & Legal Studies* 9 (3): 323–345. https://doi.org/10.1177/096466390000900301.

Observatorio Nacional de Seguridad Ciudadana. 2013. *Percepcion de La Inseguridad y Evaluacion de Las Instituciones de Seguridad Ciudadana.* La Paz, Bolivia: Ministerio de Gobierno and Vice-ministerio de Seguridad Ciudadana.

PB, Policía Boliviana. 2009. "Diagnostico de Seguridad". PowerPoint Presentation for Training.

PB, Policía Boliviana. 2014a. *Aplicación del Modelo de Policía Comunitaria en la Policía Boliviana.* La Paz: Bolivia.

PB, Policía Boliviana. 2014b. *Modelo de Policía Comunitaria Con Enfoque de Filosofía de Trabajo En La Policía Boliviana.* Comando General de la Policia Boliviana, Direcion Nacional de Planeamiento y Operaciones.

Pratten, David, and Atreyee Sen. 2007. *Global Vigilantes.* London: Hurst.

Risør, Helene. 2010. *Violent Closures and New Openings – Civil Insecurity, Citizens and State in El Alto, Bolivia.* PhD Dissertation, Department of Anthropology, University of Copenhagen, Copenhagen. https://dignityinstitute.org/media/2066039/violent-closures-and-new-openings-risoer-h.pdf.

Rodgers, Dennis. 2006. "The State as a Gang: Conceptualizing the Governmentality of Violence in Contemporary Nicaragua". *Critique of Anthropology* 26 (3): 315–330. https://doi.org/10.1177/0308275X06066577.

Rose, Nikolas. 2000. "Government and Control". *British Journal of Criminology* 40 (2): 321–339. https://doi.org/10.1093/bjc/40.2.321.

Sassen, Saskia. 2008. "Neither Global nor National: Novel Assemblages of Territory, Authority and Rights". *Ethics & Global Politics* 1 (1–2): 61–79. https://doi.org/10.3402/egp.v1i1.1814.

Schramm, Katharina, and Kristine Krause. 2011. "Thinking Through Political Subjectivity". *African Diaspora* 4 (2): 115–134. https://doi.org/10.1163/187254611X607741.

Sharma, Aradhana, and Akhil Gupta, eds. 2006. *The Anthropology of the State: A Reader.* Blackwell Readers in Anthropology 9. Malden and Oxford: Blackwell Publishing.

Primary data

Gonzalo Choque, 26/1/14, Interview, Cotahuma, La Paz.
Group interview 29/10/14, Interview with Roselyn, Carmen and Juan, Tembladerani, La Paz.
Jorge, 26/1/14, Interview, Cotahuma, La Paz.
Marcos Guzman, 24/1/14, Interview, Tembladerani, La Paz.
Workshop 21/10/14, Observation at Workshop on Citizen Security, Cotahuma, La Paz.

7   Border control and blurred responsibilities at the airport

Perle Møhl

In the main office of the Border Police HQ of Copenhagen Airport, a screen presenting a black and white still-image of the border zone floor becomes animated when a person moves into the area. "3D people tracking sensors" in the ceiling identify a presence and a small white dot starts moving across the image. If the person queues up in front of the manual passport control, the dot turns bright red. If the person slows down by the ABC (Automated Border Control), the dot turns blue. White is movement, movement is good. At present, the many red and blue dots have turned into big blobs, indicating that too many people are queuing in the passport control instead of lingering in the shopping areas or reaching their flights (Figure 7.1). But in the Police HQ, no one looks at the screen, except the anthropologist, fascinated by the aesthetics of the imagery, the small moving dots that change colour, and by the fact that the border control guards are themselves being controlled. The border guards, on the other hand, don't need the screen to know when people are crowding, they can hear it through the thin walls, see it from the "aquarium" and sense the bustle. But the red and blue dots are registered and audited in the offices of "CPH Airport", the private company owning and running the entire airport complex, and the data will be used in the next negotiations with police management and Frontex about increasing flow and reducing retention on the Schengen border.

Introduction

Border Security at Copenhagen Airport is maintained on a daily basis through the activities, intents and perspectives of a multiple and unstable assemblage of public and private actors and technologies. Two opposed types of motivations play the leading roles in this work: on the one hand, securing the national and Schengen borders against what are defined as intruders and threats and, on the other, a general pursuit of economic advantage and profit. Security plays a part in both, in itself becoming a negotiable commodity. The airport is a privileged site for analysing the blurring of responsibilities, decision-making and ongoing negotiations between different parties, because border security is produced by both public and private actors, and because the economic and the security stakes in this place are so

Figure 7.1 "Flow detection" monitoring of the border control zone, CPH Airport

obviously entwined and guide most interactions, as also exemplified by both Lyon's and Salter's analysis of airport security and surveillance (Lyon 2006, 2008; Salter 2008). Nevertheless, other stakes and motivations also clearly make their way into the functioning of the border security assemblage, both on the floor in the day-to-day management and production of security and control, and in the delocalised corridors of political and lobby negotiations between the various national, supranational and economic stakeholders. The interplay between diverse interests and motivations is furthermore highly unstable in that a multitude of phenomena and transformations continually come into play at all levels of the assemblage, in accordance with Deleuze and Guattari's notion of it (1980). This makes the discernment of the processes and of the assemblage itself quite obtuse to the anthropologist's eye and other senses, and thus also quite difficult to maintain in a stable, textual form.

Blurring in this assemblage has two different facets. For one, there is a *structural* blurring: it is never really clear which *actors* are involved in border security measures and to what degree. Furthermore, the very *often-conflicting agendas and interests* of the involved actors are blurred, appearing on the surface as a coherent and harmonic border security apparatus. I describe this blurring of actors and interests as structural and the chapter starts by outlining the main stakeholders that produce border control and security at Copenhagen Airport, and the often-conflicting agendas that amalgamate and become indistinct in the daily application of human and technological measures of border security. A second type of blurring occurs in the particular instances where control authority is allocated, notably in every instance where a technology or a border guard decides whether to let someone pass or not. The chapter examines two such instances of control where the actual processes of decision-making and allocation of responsibilities and authority are blurred. The examples concern, for one, the negotiations for setting an acceptable threshold for facial recognition in an Automated Border Control technology, and, secondly, the discretionary work of individual border guards in the profiling of passengers and the detection of potential threats. In both cases, I argue, these processes of decision-making constitute a blurring of border security by delocalising, internalising and individuating the border – respectively *into* the machine and *into* the individual border guard. So where one type of blurring concerns the unstable constituents of the assemblage, the other type concerns the blurring of the decisional actions it produces.

Borders, border studies and blurred assemblages

In the emergent field of critical border studies, borders are not only conceptualised as inherently geographical and physical sites of deterrence but are also seen as ephemerally enacted through a wide range of encounters and connections, notably in and between databases, ID documents, EU regulations, consulate visa redactions, migrant practices, as well as being inscribed in the bodies of travellers themselves (Adey 2009; Amoore 2006; Bigo 2002). When thinking through the eclectic notion of the assemblage, I however acknowledge that border making also does *take place*, localised in daily activities and encounters of various human and non-human agents, whether in passport controls, at airport counters or in asylum screening units. And this is indeed where an anthropological approach may be at its best, by bringing forth insights about the direct inter-human and human-technological workings of border production and management. A look into the everyday routines, happenstances and malfunctions of border guarding and the many actors that go into producing security on borders and producing secure borders, offers the opportunity to refine what by a more overall approach might somewhat hurriedly be described as a well-oiled and proficient system. As we shall see, the border assemblage is not a contradiction-less consistent monolithic whole, operated from far-away centres of computerised algorithmic intelligence, as other researchers of border production and security systems have also noted (e.g. Andrejevic and Gates 2014; Tsianos and Kuster 2016). When looking in more detail at the border security assemblage, it becomes apparent that it is instead composed of contradictory flows and desires, inconsistencies and absurdities.

Furthermore, the border security assemblage is constellated of an incessant stream of "small decisions" that are "conditioned, but not completely predetermined" (Rabinow 2004, 63, in Rheinberger 2009, 7), motivated and instantiated by individual and collegial interpretations of regulations and laws, as well as by affect (Adey 2009), by algorithms, and by externalisations and contrasting desires. I therefore argue that blurring in the border security assemblage arises in this *lack* of overarching predetermination and coherence, and in the operation of control though a series of infinitely small decisions, both human and technological.

Fieldwork on the border

The analysis in this chapter is based on fieldwork in Copenhagen Airport over a period of five months during 2016–2017. During this fieldwork, I accompanied police and civil border guards from the Airport Border Guard Police Unit of Copenhagen Police that secure the Schengen border. For one, I sat in with the border guards as they surveyed the ABC (Automated Border Control) eGates. This implied ensuring that the automation was working, scrutinising travellers, following the passport and facial controls on a screen, overruling or "helping" the system when it had "difficulties" recognising travellers or for other reasons did not open the eGates' glass doors, and making informed judgements when there were "hits" between controlled traveller IDs and the different national, European and international police and Schengen databases that the recognition system was linked up to. Secondly, I sat in with agents that manually controlled passports and visas of travellers leaving for or arriving from non-Schengen countries. Thirdly, I followed the police agents when they made "random sampling" controls at intra-Schengen flights arriving from so-called "high-risk" European countries. I furthermore participated in the two daily briefings of the border police unit, in the short training sessions dispensed by the "DocuUnit" specialised in document fraud and falsification, and in the surveillance of various sites via CCTV and other types of screen work. Through this work, I also got insights into the general border security work undertaken by private stakeholders, the diverse surveillance technologies at play and the work of the two private companies that produce, install and maintain the ABC eGates.

I did not conduct formal interviews. Rather, I discussed procedures and events over lunch and talked with border guards while we watched people, screens and movement, interrogating together what we saw. I participated in meetings and briefings, and I was myself interviewed about my work by management, by unionists, by airport security, all producing insightful materials about how *they* saw *their* work. I took handwritten notes, both by preference and because any digital technology would be seen as too intrusive, even though the field was full of such technologies. I also took occasional photos with my phone. Everyone had a phone on them; it was an accepted work tool, part of the uniform.

During fieldwork, I wore a police sign and was therefore addressed by travellers as a police officer. I observed the work of the border control agents I accompanied and took notes, and travellers appeared to classify me as a higher-ranking officer in the police hierarchy since I was ostensibly overseeing and controlling the agents. This was an unusual and challenging position to be in and a predicament that I continually analysed and tried to learn from as a constituent of the border world itself. Indeed, in some people's eyes, I *was* the border. This set some very particular frames for the field-work, notably concerning the temporal and spatial outreach of what I could perceive of the travellers' routes, hitherto and beyond this space, the nature of what they told me, depending on how they positioned me, and how I in turn could address them. In sum, the span of my perspective and thus knowledge about the travellers was narrowed down to what a police officer would hear. Indeed, as I have noted elsewhere, it is "what one participates in that becomes one's field, one's empirical object", and thus what one can get to know something about, and not the other way around (Møhl 2011, 243). It was frustrating at first but also an important acknowledgement about my analytical object and scope: I was here to get insight into police and border guard procedures and perspectives, and not to obtain an all-embracing over-view of the border world nor of particular migrant itineraries and dreams for the future. Indeed, this was the position I had allotted myself and that the police management had surprisingly willingly allowed me to take up.

The border security stakeholders at CPH Airport

At Copenhagen Airport, a complex assemblage of public and private stake-holders and a multitude of minute daily human and technological actors and actions go into the daily production of border security, working through a *structural blurring* that makes it difficult to discern the distribution of authority and the conflicting agendas.

Copenhagen Airport is the main Danish airport, but also serves as an entry-point into Scandinavia and functions as the international airport for the greater part of Southern Sweden, besides constituting a Schengen entry point. The public security actors are of various national and international constellations: the Danish state represented by Copenhagen Border Police and the DocuUnit of the National Police are in charge of border control and general security, and Frontex, an EU agency, coordinates national bor-der control and carries out sometimes unannounced checks at the airport to audit the efficiency of the national border units. Alongside these public actors, a variety of private actors contribute to the security assemblage: The airport itself is run by "CPH Airports" (CPH), a predominantly private company currently owned in majority by a Canadian holder. CPH and its sub-group, CPH Security, are in charge of all entry and exit security checks of goods and persons at the airport.[1] A multitude of airline and security companies, as well as the many retailers and food stalls also carry out large measures of security and movement control and contribute to the overall security assemblage. A range of private companies provides and maintains the wide variety of technologies of control employed by both public and private actors. Outsourcing is thus an important factor of the assemblage, entangling connections and further blurring the interplay of border secu-rity practices at the airport. This to a large extent obstructs an overview of the measures of coercion at play (Adey 2009; Bloom and Risse 2014).

Furthermore, a variety of security and border control technologies and practices operate both on location and at a distance as externalisations, both through data exchanges and as actual deterritorialised control activities outside the airport. So the assemblage is far-reaching, obtuse and of many formats and materialities.

Although these actors constitute an assemblage of "heterogeneous objects" that "'work' together as a functional entity" (Patton 1994, 158, in Haggerty and Ericson 2000, 608), they are also aligned by opposing interests and desires, notably flow vs. efficient control and profit vs. legal action, as we shall see. Furthermore, if the assemblage produces operations that momentarily capture and fixate flows (ibid.), that fixation is itself a sight of friction and continued negotiation between all these different private and public actors. From the vantage point of their different desires – legal, practical, economic, temporal, individual – they produce different forms of security, and those desires and the ensuing operations are more or less tangible and simple to detect, indeed often quite obscure, hidden and in some cases, themselves only arduously subject to external scrutiny and control, notably by state, EU and NGO agencies.

With this outline of the actors and agendas, we can now look closer at the allocation of authority through particular instances where blurring *takes place* and is situated. To do so, I will first present the overall work of border control at the Schengen airport border.

Controlling the Schengen border

Airplanes flying to CPH from non-Schengen countries arrive at Pier C, coming mainly from the Middle East and Turkey, Asia, the US and from European non-Schengen member states, such as the UK. Of the roughly 80,000 persons who daily travel in and out of CPH Airport, 19,500 cross the Schengen border. As a heightened security measure, all documents are currently scanned, meaning that no discrimination based on profiling takes place. Border control is done by police officers and by first-line civil officers who have gone through a nine weeks training programme. The civil officers have only a controlling and not an executive faculty, and call in second-line police officers in case of database "hits" or questions of possible document or identity fraud. But in the checking booths, they do exactly the same work as the police officers. Because of both carrier responsibility and ID verification at check-in, persons who arrive at the airport border almost always have documents. Only in the rare cases where people seek international protection do they arrive at the border without documents to show. The work therefore mainly consists of checking that 1) the presented document is valid and not counterfeit or forged, 2) the holder is also the person presented in the document, i.e. not travelling with someone else's genuine document, called "impersonation" (Frontex 2013) and 3) the document and visa are valid for passage across this particular border and into Denmark and Schengen, both for Schengen citizens and third-country nationals with Schengen member-state residence permits.

The people who are intercepted at the border fall into roughly three categories: persons travelling on visas or identity cards that do not permit travel into or out of Denmark or Schengen (by far the biggest group);[2] persons who have a national or international arrest warrant against them; and persons travelling on another person's genuine documents (currently the most commonly reported document fraud).[3] Besides such cases, certain persons are also under national or international surveillance, their moves being "discretely monitored", which means that the border guards note down their passage but do not apprehend or engage in any direct interaction with them. Both for "discretely monitored" persons and arrest warrants, the scanned document will give rise to a "hit" in one of the connected databases. But many "hits" concern persons who are wanted but for whom the identification elements are incomplete, leading to a long series of "false hits", e.g. because a surname or part of a document number coincide with the traveller's. In all cases, a police officer will inspect the ID of the traveller and determine whether the person in question can access (or leave) Danish/Schengen territory or should be held back for further inspection, be arrested or simply denied passage.

At Copenhagen Airport, a series of Automated Border Control (ABC) eGates have recently been installed, with the main goal of heightening security from the standpoint that facial recognition technologies and biometric passports provide more efficient forms of control. Another motivation for installing the costly technology is to comply with the airport's request for a higher flow at the border. But in fact, according to the police officers operating on the border, the eGates are not necessarily quicker. They furthermore imply a deskillment of the human control agents with the risk of replacing them with more machines to cut down on wage expenses, as the union representatives complain. Finally, the algorithmic settings of the eGates can be – and are – negotiated between police agencies, CPH Airport and the technology developer, *Vision-Box*, to heighten flow, notably by lowering the threshold for the required match between the ID-photo and the live facial capture at the ABC eGates, as we shall see.

In the following I will examine the work of the ABC eGates and the kind of blurring it represents in the production of border security. This analysis will be followed by the description of the random identity checks that border police guards are requested to carry out at intra-Schengen flights, looking for what is defined as "high-risk" travellers. In both cases, the blurring arises through mechanisms of dislocation of border security from the actual border when control and responsibility are projected respectively into an algorithmic figure and onto the individual border guard's subjective discretional interpretation and judgement, thereby obfuscating both the actual acts of decision-making and their incentives, as well as the respective influences and opposing interests of the multiple constituents of the security assemblage.

Case 1: human-technological border work

At the ABC eGates, Sandra, a civil border control agent, is checking incoming passengers from non-Schengen countries, currently from a US and a UK flight. To pass through the eGate, the passengers need to have a biometric EU (or EEA) "ePassport". The British are good at passing quickly, Sandra says. They're used to facial recognition because they have the same kind of machines at Heathrow. The passengers queue up in front of the six active gates, waiting behind a yellow line. When one has passed, a green light invites the next passenger to approach and scan his or her passport. After a while the first glass door opens and lets the passenger enter the small enclosure between the two glass doors where he/she is invited to move up to the facial scan camera and stand on the two yellow footprints on the floor. A second-line police officer steps in to indicate the right position, "if they are fooling around in there", as he says. "Stand still, not too close". "Take off your glasses". "Take off your hat". "Remove your veil". "Look at the camera".

Sandra sits in the tall glass booth that gives an overview of the six eGates. From here she surveys people moving into the ABC zone, the persons queuing and the persons inside the six eGates – scrutinising their faces and their behaviour, checking if they suddenly change route and choose the manual passport control, keeping an eye on her screens and communicating by radio with the second-line officer and her colleagues in the other booths. She has two screens. One relates the operations and images of the ABC, how it is functioning, how each facial recognition scores, whether there are problems, for example if the passport photo and the facial scan don't match, or if the machine indicates that there are two persons in the gate. She overrides the ABC and opens the exit gate manually if she can see "it is getting confused" and if she can identify the reasons – a person with a lot of hand luggage that is identified as two, or a person that the machine cannot recognise whereas Sandra can easily make the match between the chip and passport images on the screen and the actual face she can see through her window. She is "learning to see in 2D", she says, like the machine, comparing a 2D screen photo to an actual physical 3D face. The other screen on the table indicates that the connection to the different national and international police databases is up and running and gives alerts when there are hits – correspondences – between the ABC information and the databases. If so, the second gate does not open automatically and a fat red edge and a red triangle with a "!" appears on the image on the ABC screen. In this case, Sandra reads the information provided by the databases, assesses the nature of the correspondence, e.g. between information about an Interpol search warrant and the information provided on the person in the ABC eGate via the passport. If in doubt, she calls upon the second-line officer to make an assessment and decide which action to take. With most cases, the "hit" is a false hit. But once in a while a passenger is pulled aside for further inquiry or held back if formally identified as wanted or, for example, as having to hand in a driver's licence that has been withdrawn. As such, the ABC also works as a justified site of control of offences not related to border crossing.

Sandra moves over to the outgoing ABC eGate. A person of what she identifies as of East African origin arrives at the ABC and stops to look. He then moves over to the manual passport control and she calls her colleagues there and tells them that he has moved away from the ABC eGate. As it turns out, he has come in from Italy and is trying to take a plane to the UK on an EU passport that is not his own. He probably decided not to risk the facial control, since the machine is better at recognising African faces than Europeans are, she says. She asks me why that is, thinking there might be a "natural", anthropological explanation to it. She tells me that on her guard last week an airline security agent called in the police because a traveller had been stopped from boarding a Heathrow flight when trying to travel with another person's passport. The DocuUnit apprehended the traveller and ran him through the ABC three times, and he almost passed once. "So sometimes the machine works better, sometimes the human eye does".

Over lunch I ask one of Sandra's colleagues what he thinks about the ABC and if he sometimes works there. "No". He doesn't like it; he prefers human contact. Another officer declares he also dislikes the ABC: "The machine can't think. It's stupid and can only obey orders given by humans. It can't think ahead. I have intuition, I'm creative". And, he says, if the bosses or the airport company for some reason want a higher flow, they can just turn down the machine's vigilance with a click of a mouse, while "They can't turn down mine".

Technological negotiations as a blurring of responsibilities

When Sandra sits in her booth repeatedly looking up, out and down – up at people's faces, out over the queues and down at her screens – and taking small decisions every time she hits a button or clicks with the mouse, she is in the middle of a wide and complex assemblage where a lot of other actors of various kinds play out important roles in the control of the border. As mentioned, assemblages emerge "out of a lot of small decisions" (Rabinow 2004, in Rheinberger 2009, 7). I have already described the many public, private, material and immaterial actors that co-constitute the assemblage, and Sandra's and her second-line officer's actions also form minute parts of the ongoing border security assemblage. The framework for their decisions is set up by CPH Airport, by Danish Police management, by the Danish government, by EU and Frontex, and the many laws and directives they all produce; by the wide range of technologies involved in the security control; by the intentions, possibilities and interventions of the passing travellers; by the airline companies who maintain their own borders to avoid carrier responsibility fines and secure their flights; by the many private security companies they all engage; by the technology developers and maintenance groups, both private and in-house; by the weather and the time of year – in summer on sunny days, the ABC camera gets sun "in its eyes" and "can't see well"; by travel trends and economic fluctuations; by union policies, and collegial connections and considerations, by their daily wellbeing and health-conditions; and by the interplay of all those innumerable factors and many more. There is overtly intentional conditioning – the design of the environment, protocols for action, assignment of authority – but there are very few of those intentional conditionings that actually turn into predictable and predetermined outputs.

In this blurred configuration, we can nevertheless determine some of the conditionings that define *what it takes* for the glass doors of the ABC eGates to open and let a traveller through. This has to do with negotiating the setting of the required threshold for the facial recognition technology: CPH sets up flow detection monitoring screens in the police HQ on the border so the police officers in charge can see when they are slowing down the passenger flow, retaining potential customers who should instead be retained – and tempted – in the shopping areas. On the background of a black-and-white photo of the border zone, retained passengers appear in real-time as small red dots, rapidly accumulating into a red mass when flow in the manual passport control is low. People moving are presented as neutral white dots and people waiting at the ABC are represented as blue dots. CPH not only makes this "dot stream" (Xovis 2017) available to the border police, as we saw above, but also transforms the dots and their respective colours into figures and graphs. They use these audits to calculate actual flow and staffing needs and allot passenger assistants ("frogs" as they are called by police staff because of their green t-shirts). More importantly, they use them to negotiate with the border police about spatial organisation, border guard staffing and in their requests for the acquisition of new technological equipment as well as the running of current technology.

The white dots moving on the monitors constitute instances of "blank figures" that can become anything (Serres 1991; Svendsen 2011), bodies without ID. They are even merchandised as "anonymous" by the developer (Xovis 2017). What counts (is counted) is not *who* they are, but what they *might do*, imbued as they are with very different types of potential: to the airport company and many shop holders, they constitute potential customers moving towards goods of consumption – when not upheld in the passport control ("red", "blue"). To the border police, the blank figures are uncertain and undetermined presences, possible threats to security until firmly ID'ed.

Police management and unions negotiate with CPH and with the private Portuguese firm *Vision-Box* and its Danish maintenance provider, *Biometric Solutions*, about the settings (the system acceptance threshold) of the necessary score level of facial recognition in the ABC, in compliance with loose Frontex recommendations. The "dot streams" are used by CPH in these negotiations. The goal is to find a balance between flow and retention, between false positives and false negatives. Frontex recommends a facial recognition score of, say 50, whereas CPH wants to lower it to 42 to heighten flows.[4] Copenhagen Police wants to comply with Frontex recommendations and set the threshold at 50 for higher security, but the maintenance provider sets the threshold somewhere in between, for the moment. It is difficult – for all involved – to determine who has actually made the decision, but the border guards can see on the screen that people now pass with a lower recognition score – and they know that a technician from *Biometric Solutions* did indeed change the settings with the click of a mouse. In this negotiation, the threshold level, one simple number – e.g. "46" – comes to contain and encapsulate all the divergent desires and their ongoing negotiations, transforming threats, regulations, security levels, document fraud, state policies, EU directives as well as seamlessness, flow, travel experience, pleasure, human rights, and so on, into *one single figure*. Click! Every time a person passes through the ABC eGate, several facial scan samples are made and run through the system while the doors stay closed in both ends. The algorithmically configured results are held up against the template in the passport and if the magic figure, e.g. 47 or 88, is reached, the exit door opens automatically. The figure is somewhat arbitrary because it is the result of opposing forces but comes to encapsulate and actualise the required level of recognition, i.e. how much one is required to resemble the ID-photo of oneself in order to be considered oneself – a match! – and for the door to open.

The threshold figure is so unequivocal – it is a simple number – yet constitutes an effective blurring. For one, it is a figure that many of the involved can't *see*, suspended as it is between all these different actors and their ongoing negotiations to find a middle ground between their differing agendas. And it is a blurring – opacification – by virtue of its *oneness* that signals consensus and thus *nullifies* all the existing differentials, tensions and contentions. But they are not resolved; they are simply glossed over. And every time the threshold figure strikes again and the door opens, the nullification of contentions and the blurring of responsibilities is replayed. Again, the "blank figure" or joker, here in the form of the threshold, represses all contention, taking it "to zero" (Serres 1991). Quite inversely, however, every time the white dots on the Police HQ monitors become blue, they effectively display and reiterate the existence of discordance and conflicting desires.

The airline companies are ambivalent, both interested in getting passengers through border control quickly so they don't derange flight schedules and on assuring both flight security and ID control, because they risk a fine and having to fly people back to their site of embarkation. They therefore do their own ID checks upon boarding. This is yet another example of decision-making responsibility being indirectly allocated to singular actors within the assemblage, making it more difficult to control and critique. But if the distribution of responsibilities is blurred, the assemblage is in no way a well-oiled machine. On the contrary, it is composed of diverging desires and objectives, conflicting interests and actions, and national and international and profit-seeking wishes, where specific actors often are pointed out by the others, getting fines or admonitions for mistakes and miscalculations that might be attributed to them. It is not a coherent pre-programmed whole, but a nervous and constantly fluctuating constellation of interconnected moves and desires, collisions and friction operating "across difference and distance" (Tsing 2005, 2), and appearing to both participating and external actors are opaque and blurred.

Case 2: controlling "high-risk" flights

Border police officers regularly carry out random security and ID checks at flights arriving from Schengen countries. Such random checks are permitted within EU regulations under certain conditions, namely that they *are* random, which by the border police is defined as non-permanent and concerning only a certain amount of flights per week. The randomness in itself constitutes a blurring of responsibility, since all decisions are discretionary, taken by individual police officers without formal orders or protocols. The blurring thus takes the form of an individuation of border control, transferring – allocating – responsibility to the individual border guard. These checks are firmly audited by the police management, both to monitor that the work is being done and to document the number of checks in case of Frontex controls – even if the border police's work is not "to produce figures", as a police officer in charge stated. The checks are carried out by armed police officers and not civilian agents, because they are "out in the open".

Walking to Pier F where we will await the arrival of a low-cost plane from an Italian city, I accompany Hans, a short and sturdily built police agent and his new female colleague who is carrying out a random check for the first time. He is explaining the principles to her as well as the incidents with passengers that such checks sometimes give rise to. "We're looking for illegal immigrants. So we don't stop Mr. and Mrs. Hansen". While we wait, I ask him how he can see whom to pick out if he is not allowed to stop everyone. He has some tricks, he says. He can for example detect undocumented Afghan men, i.e. people who haven't been here before or don't live here, without checking their passports. "They try to blend in but always look sort of inept-smart. You know, jeans with holes in them. Sunglasses. And there's always something with the shoes, they never fit the rest. Too fancy".

The flight arrives and they take up position at the exit of the gangway. Almost all passengers are Danish tourists coming home. But four are of African origins, arriving one by one. The first two are pulled aside, and are asked to produce their documents. They don't put up any resistance. A couple of other passengers frown or slow down, but do not intervene. A third is pulled aside and a fourth passes by the officers who are occupied checking the others. All three checked have the necessary documents. Once checked, Hans smiles to them and wishes them a safe journey. He notes down the flight number and the number of checked persons on an old piece of paper so the officer on duty can enter it into "the system" and the two walk off to the other end of the airport to check a flight arriving from Athens.

"High-risk" profiling as a blurring of responsibilities

So how does the randomness and the notion of "high-risk flights" configure and blur the nature of what is going on and the "production of suspicion" (Murphy and Maguire 2015, 165)? "High-Risk" is used in a double sense by Frontex, as both a way to optimise resources by applying them to regions of "high-risk" of migration influx (Council of the European Union 2017), i.e. an organisational sense, and geographically, when referring to specific places of origin – although "high-risk" in this case ostensibly relates to routes (Kasparek 2010) and thus not to nationalities. Somewhat in accordance, at Copenhagen Airport, certain flights are defined as high-risk because they arrive from cities within Schengen that Frontex and the national authorities consider possible avenues of "illegal migrants" and refugees. They count Milan, Rome, Athens and other Greek and Italian and, to some extent, Spanish cities, i.e. intra-Schengen routes that normally are exempt of border control, but where there are high levels of arrivals of undocumented persons from the Middle East, Asia and Africa. So, when the border police randomly control such flights, i.e. submit only some flights and only some passengers to control, the notion of "high-risk" comes to relate directly to the countries of origin of the possible migrants and asylum seekers, meaning that they are in fact profiling nationalities and not just checking routes. And as a result, the persons who are effectively pulled aside when leaving the plane are all, almost per definition, people who ostensibly come from non-Schengen countries. "High-risk" thus logically, and also according to the border police officers themselves, implies that they must check *people* who "look high-risk", for example like they come in from an African country or from the Middle East. And as several officers have declared when I inquired about these practices and the meaning of "high-risk", this is paradoxical, because it makes them take decisions based on what effectively amounts to "racial profiling". So the law at the same time prohibits and actively installs a system of racial and ethnic profiling. Furthermore, even if they might want to contest the legality and ethics of these random checks and the fact that they are making them "behave racist",[5] the unit is as mentioned required to produce a certain number of random checks per week for future Frontex and management audits, producing a classical "feedback loop" logic where only certain groups are controlled and where the figures therefore concern only these groups, thereby both reinforcing and justifying future controls of the *same* target groups (cf. Fassin 2013; Holmberg 2000).

    From the perspective of a security assemblage analysis, it is the configuration of the notion of "high-risk" that merits attention, co-produced as it is by a number of different national and supranational actors that more or less overtly contribute to its meaning, leading to very particular and discriminatory effects in the control of movement and the profiling of travellers. Furthermore, the principle of "randomness" displaces the choice-making on to the individual police officers who come to determine which flights and which passengers are to be seen as "high-risk", relocating responsibility onto the notorious "sixth sense" and "gut feeling" of the individual officer, i.e. the legally installed discretion or hunch (*skøn*) (Holmberg 2000, 2003; Brouwer et al. 2017). This ultimately places any executive act within the field of subjective, intuitive and therefore impalpable, often unacknowledged and un-verbalised individual interpretation and discernment. So ultimately, "high-risk" and random checks contribute to a virtual blurring of the premises for and the production of border security at the airport.

Conclusions

The security assemblage operating on the heterogeneous border of Copenhagen Airport is made up of a complex of varying desires for both flow and retention, of contrasting political-organisational objectives and practical feasibilities. These are desires to which we have only a partial insight, both because of the transfer and blurring of responsibilities (Hönig 2014) and because of the way these desires continuously interact and contradict one another, making the functioning at every moment fluctuating and unsystematic. With Ulrich Beck's term, we could define this blurring as an "organised irresponsibility" (2009), where the definitions of high-risk and of the necessary recognition thresholds are delegated to a variety of singular actors – in the two examples, facial recognition algorithms and individual officers' discretion – that are difficultly identifiable. The recognition threshold of the ABC technology blurs the conflicts between public and private actors, as well as the unofficial negotiations between their conflicting agendas, while its oneness ostensibly signifies a perfect consensus between the actors. The "high-risk" notion blurs the responsibility of implementing national and EU migration policies by assigning responsibility and decisions to individual officers and their personal tactics, while imposing certain selective logics. The notion comes to produce very problematic procedures of discrimination, also in the eyes of those who are implementing them in their daily work.

Such blurring makes the security assemblage difficult to assess and to control. No one ever really knows who is involved in producing border security in the different sites and how strongly they influence the procedures according to their variegated agendas. This is a predicament for both authoritative agencies on various levels, for NGOs wishing to protect human mobility and privacy rights (Bloom and Risse 2014) and for individuals trying to make their way through the security assemblage.

It is also a predicament for the researcher wishing to gain an insight into the current state of affairs of local border work. But by following specific procedures in the daily work of border security agents who individually take a multitude of "small decisions" in their choice-making and interaction with the automated machines, it does become clear that there is no overarching predetermined and coherent border security machine at work. Some particular lines of force nevertheless stand out, both about the nature of the blurredness and about the redistribution of responsibilities, as the analysis of the examples has shown.

And finally, it is a predicament for the people and actors engaged in the daily work on the floor. The border guards feel their authority is being undercut and their know-how is waning as they become deskilled by machines that take over the scrutinising, that can only recognise and not cognise and that can't think creatively. The machine does not work through discretion, but acts on a clear albeit arbitrarily set figure, and its vigilance level can be lowered by the click of a mouse. Who actually sets that figure is never really clear. The border guards can turn off the machine – and they sometimes do when it starts "glitching", malfunctions in one gate "spreading to the others like a virus" – but when it is running, they can only assist it. The airline companies administer the work of border control without clear orders and with the risk of penalties if they transport persons who are not admissible. And travellers end up either caught in awkward and secluded locations or without the possibility to ask for the international protection to which they would be entitled, and the organisations that are trying to ensure that such rights are protected stand helpless. Possibly, and not surprisingly, the only actors who seem to pull an advantage from the incongruities, the blurring and the lack of clear responsibilities are the private contractors who carry out preventive control for the airline companies, the airport holdings that own and design airport spaces as vast shopping malls and sites of leisure, pleasure and new shopping experiences, as well as the private agencies that provide the vast array of costly technological infrastructures applied in security, surveillance, flow monitoring and border control. Security and border control certainly does slow down the flow of bodies-as-potential-customers – turning mobile white dots into red blurbs – and thereby blemishes the performance of the airport as a site of pleasure and seamless movement provided by a coherent body. But going through security and border control at the same time becomes – and is commodified as – a reassuring and selective quality inherent to that exclusive pleasure and movement.

Acknowledgements

The research project, *Biometric technologies and the enskillment of vision in border control*, with fieldworks in Denmark, Gibraltar and Spain, has been financed by the Velux Foundation, and I would like to thank the foundation for their support. The project is part of a larger collaborative project, *Biometric Border Worlds*.

Notes

1 CPH Airports employs ca. 2,500 persons, of which ca. 1,200 alone work at CPH Security.
2 Defined as "unauthorised secondary movement of third-country nationals" (European Commission 2017). Such cases also include visa overstay.
3 Among travellers leaving Denmark/Schengen there are also many cases of overstay, either concerning visas or temporary EU residence permits. In such cases, there is a certain ambivalence among the guards about whether to let them leave the country "a bit late" or to stop them for offence, depending on the duration of the overstay. This ambivalence is related to the perplexing notion of individual intuitive discretion – *skøn* – that Danish police officers are required to apply in their decision-making (Holmberg 2000) and that will be discussed further on.
4 The recognition (or similarity) score refers to the similarity between the features of respectively the face in the ABC eGate and in the passport photo. There is rarely a 100 percent match, but photo and face should match to a certain degree, indicating the accepted "recognition threshold". The threshold and thus the required similarity score can be raised or lowered, making it more or less easy to pass. The figures on the screen range between 0 and 100, but do not indicate a percentage, but a score, as a *Vision-Box* representative repeatedly stated when the border guards talked of percent. Calling them percent, as in "you only need to look 49 percent like your passport photo", is probably considered by developers and policy-makers as a misguided indication of low border security, as in "only half good enough".
5 As one interlocutor despairingly noted, "If I wasn't a racist before, this work is making me into one". What she was referring to was not that her personal opinion vis-à-vis certain ethnic groups was changing, but that she was being asked to apply higher vigilance and suspicion to certain groups than to others, in what one could thus define as a case of "systemic racism".

References

Adey, Peter. 2009. "Facing Airport Security: Affect, Biopolitics, and the Preemptive Securitisation of the Mobile Body". *Environment and Planning D: Society and Space* 27: 274–296.

Amoore, Louise. 2006. "Biometric Borders: Governing Mobilities in the War on Terror". *Political Geography* 25: 336–351.

Andrejevic, Mark, and Kelly Gates. 2014. "Big Data Surveillance: Introduction". *Surveillance & Society* 12 (2): 185–196.

Beck, Ulrich. 2009. "Critical Theory of World Risk Society: A Cosmopolitan Vision". *Constellations* 16 (1): 3–22.

Bigo, Didier. 2002. "Security and Immigration: Toward a Critique of the Governmentality of Unease". *Alternatives* 27: 63–92.

Bloom, Tendayi, and Verena Risse. 2014. "Examining Hidden Coercion at State Borders: Why Carrier Sanctions Cannot Be Justified". *Ethics & Global Politics* 7 (2): 65–82.

Brouwer, Jelmer, Maartje van der Woude, and Joanne van der Leun. 2017. "(Cr)immigrant Framing in Border Areas: Decision-making Processes of Dutch Border Police Officers". *Policing and Society* 28 (4): 448–463.

Council of the European Union. "Frontex Draft Programming Document 2018–2020". www.statewatch.org/news/2017/feb/eu-frontex-work-programme-2018-20.pdf, accessed June 26, 2017.

Deleuze, Gilles, and Félix Guattari. 1980. *Mille plateaux (Capitalisme et schizophré-nie II)*. Paris: Éditions de Minuit.

European Commission. 2017. "Commission Recommendation of 12.5.2017 on Proportionate Police Checks and Police Cooperation in the Schengen Area". www.statewatch.org/news/2017/may/eu-com-recommendation-police-checks-final-17-2923.pdf, accessed July 16, 2017.

Fassin, Didier. 2013. *Enforcing Order: An Ethnography of Urban Policing*. Cambridge: Polity Press.

Frontex. 2013. *Frontex Evaluation Report 2013 – Joint Operation METEOR 2013 – Air Border Cooperation*. Warsaw: Frontex.

Haggerty, Kevin D., and Richard V. Ericson. 2000. "The Surveillant Assemblage". *British Journal of Sociology* 51 (4): 605–622.

Holmberg, Lars. 2000. "Discretionary Leniency and Typological Guilt: Results From a Danish Study of Police Discretion". *Journal of Scandinavian Studies in Criminology and Crime Prevention* 1 (2): 179–194.

Holmberg, Lars. 2003. *Policing Stereotypes: A Qualitative Study of Police Work in Denmark*. Glienicke and Madison: Galda + Wilch Verlag.

Hönig, Patrick. 2014. "States, Borders and the State of Exception: Framing the Unauthorised Migrant in Europe". *Etnofoor* 26 (1): 125–145.

Kasparek, Bernd. 2010. "Borders and Populations in Flux: Frontex's Place in the European Union's Migration Management". In *The Politics of International Migration Management*, edited by M. Geiger and A. Pécoud, 119–140. London: Palgrave Macmillan UK.

Lyon, David. 2006. "Airport Screening, Surveillance, and Social Sorting: Canadian Responses to 9/11 in Context". *Canadian Journal of Criminology and Criminal Justice* 48 (3): 397–411.

Lyon, David. 2008. "Filtering Flows, Friends, and Foes: Global Surveillance". In *Politics at the Airport*, edited by Mark B. Salter, 29–49. Minneapolis: University of Minnesota Press.

Møhl, Perle. 2011. "Mise en scène, Knowledge and Participation: Considerations of a Filming Anthropologist". *Visual Anthropology* 24 (3): 227–245.

Murphy, Eileen, and Mark Maguire. 2015. "Speed, Time and Security: Anthropological Perspectives on Automated Border Control". *Etnofoor* 27 (2): 157–177.

Patton, Paul. 1994. "MetamorphoLogic: Bodies and Powers in A Thousand Plateaus". *Journal of the British Society for Phenomenology* 25(2): 157–69.

Rabinow, Paul. 2004. Anthropologie des Zeitgenössischen. In *Anthropologie der Vernunft: Studien zu Wissenschaft und Lebensführung*, 56–65. Suhrkamp: Frankfurt am Main.

Rheinberger, Hans-Jörg. 2009. "Recent Science and Its Exploration: The Case of Molecular Biology". *Studies in History and Philosophy of Biological and Biomedical Sciences* 40: 6–12.

Salter, Mark B. 2008. "The Global Airport: Managing Space, Speed, and Security". In *Politics at the Airport*, edited by Mark B. Salter, 1–28. Minneapolis: University of Minnesota Press.

Serres, Michel. 1991. *Rome: The Book of Foundations*. Stanford: Stanford University Press.

Svendsen, Mette N. 2011. "Articulating Potentiality: Notes on the Delineation of the Blank Figure in Human Embryonic Stem Cell Research". *Cultural Anthropology* 26 (3): 414–437.

Tsianos, Vassilis S., and Brigitta Kuster. 2016. "How to Liquefy a Body on the Move: Eurodac and the Making of the European Digital Border". In *EU Borders and Shifting Internal Security*, edited by R. Bossong and H. Carrapico, 45–63. Cham: Springer International Publishing.

Tsing, Anna. 2005. *Friction: An Ethnography of Global Connection.* Princeton: Princeton University Press.

Xovis. www.xovis.com/en/xovis/, accessed August 18, 2017.

Afterword

Rivke Jaffe

This volume seeks to tackle head on those many contexts in which the entanglement of different security actors, rationalities, objects and aesthetic markers blurs distinctions between categories such as public and private, state and non-state, commercial and voluntary. The editors and the authors of the empirical chapters explore how this blurring is produced through performances of security, which systemic factors drive such performances, and what their political effects are. Why do various types of security professionals, or self-identified protectors, actively engage in practices that make them hard to separate from one another? Is this production of indistinction driven by the individual or collective motivations of these professionals? Is it shaped by larger political and economic shifts? Is it contested or encouraged by the various publics witnessing these performances? Who is invested in keeping boundaries clearly recognisable and who seeks to actively remove such clarity? Drawing on ethnographic research, the authors take an in-depth look at how the blurring of security-related categories and roles takes shape in everyday life and in mundane security encounters, and what this means to the various people involved. In addition, they attend to the non-human elements that mediate security performances, showing how key forms of materiality – weapons, technological devices, cars, uniforms, documents – contribute to generating uncertainty about who is who, and what is what.

By "sticking with the blur", the editors and authors build on and extend previous work that has focused on the privatisation and pluralisation of security provision. Enrique Desmond Arias and Daniel M. Goldstein's (2010) important work on "violent pluralism" has emphasised the work cut out for anthropologists in analysing the co-existence of multiple armed groups, from police and military, to paramilitary groups and vigilantes, to private security companies and neighbourhood watches. This book, however, moves beyond the idea of pluralism to question the neat separation of actors and categories terms such as privatisation and pluralisation apply. In addition, by drawing on socio-material approaches often grouped under the label of "assemblage", the book draws on the emergent more-than-human sensibility within the anthropology of security, while insisting on an attentiveness to the everyday politics of these assemblages that is often missing in less ethnographic studies. In addition, it directs our attention to how these politics take shape outside of Europe and North America, regions that still form the dominant geographical basis for theorisation in mainstream security studies.

The approach developed in this book also speaks directly to conversations in political and legal anthropology and urban studies. In concentrating on how the boundaries between taken-for-granted categories such as public and private are destabilised through security practices, various chapters tie to broader political and legal anthropological discussions on governmentality beyond the state. The production of "stateness" is an important question in such discussions, and the domain of security – and specifically including the perspectives of security professionals themselves – provides an important vantage point for studying this. More specifically, the book connects to work on legality versus legitimacy, for instance Alan Smart's (2012) suggestion that we attend to the many shades of grey that fall within the spectrum of legality versus illegality, emphasising the processes of lightening and darkening that take place over time. In addition, the relational and processual approach the book advances ties to work within urban studies (e.g. Boudreau and Davis 2017) that has sought to trouble dominant conceptualisations of formality and informality, showing instead how what we can study are processes of formalisation and informalisation. Like the production of uncertainty described in this book, these processes of categorising "grey areas" as one extreme or the other are highly political, and often serve to legitimise systems of rule.

Security Blurs does a great job in demonstrating the similarities and differences between blurred and blurring security performances across a range of cultural and political contexts. The different chapters make critical contributions to our understanding of how, why and to what effect these "blurs" emerge. The editors' analytical distinction between the structural, performative and effective layers of observable "security acts" is a useful heuristic device (if perhaps obscuring some of the dialectical relations by which effects become structure, and implying a linearity that sits a bit uneasily with assemblage approaches). How might we move forward if we stick with the blur, but also think beyond it conceptually? What concepts might help us clarify the indistinction of security in new ways? I make two suggestions here for possible analytical avenues, thinking through and beyond "the blur".

A first proposition, drawing on science and technology studies, connects to this book's interest not only in boundary-making and unmaking, but also in materiality and technology. Carolina Frossard and I have begun to explore how we might draw on the concept "boundary objects" to understand how specific artefacts can connect public and private security professionals across the state/corporate boundary (Frossard and Jaffe 2018). Susan Star and James Griesemer (1989) developed the concept of boundary objects to refer to those adaptable epistemic artefacts that exist across intersecting social worlds, and can satisfy each of their information requirements. Such objects bridge knowledge and in so doing link different occupational communities, often with a clearly defined shared goal. In the security context such artefacts might include specific communication technology or policing databases. But as Martijn Koster (2014) suggests, material spaces – shared rooms or buildings – can have similar connective effects. Such boundary objects and boundary spaces emphasise commonality, and by so doing contribute to the blur, but they simultaneously work to highlight differences.

Various chapters in this book highlight the role of specific objects and technologies – what new insights might we gain if we approach them through the lens of boundary objects, asking how they enable shared ways of knowing and being to emerge, even as they also facilitate assertions of difference? While science and technology studies do not always make this point explicitly, this epistemic work is inherently political. The security cameras discussed by Jeremy Siegman in his chapter on a supermarket in an Israeli settlement are a good example – they allow a specific way of knowing that moves across a civilian, anti-theft mode of surveillance to a militarised logic of vision. As an artefact, the security camera can blur the difference between a manager and a military officer, yet simultaneously it may also reveal rather than merely obscure these military-civilian distinctions. The eGates, facial scan cameras and databases utilised by airport agents in Copenhagen, described by Perle Møhl, similarly connect as well as separate, disguise as well as reveal, different occupational communities, and their identities and responsibilities. And perhaps we might also conceive of the airport itself as a boundary space.

A second suggestion, also drawing on materiality and spatiality, but taking a different approach, would be to further engage security's blurring conceptually by connecting it to work on affect, and specifically recent literature on affective atmospheres. Many of the blurred and blurring security performances analysed in this book have an important affective dimension, producing and relying on embodied perceptions and emotional responses. This affective element is generally not coincidental, but pursued intentionally by security professionals who mobilise gestures, artefacts and spaces in their encounters with the public. Combinations of bodies, objects and environments can be understood as producing specific affective atmospheres (Anderson 2009), sets of material-affective relations that are atmospherically immersive, lying in between bodies, objects and material spaces. In discussing "security atmospheres", Peter Adey (2014) more specifically emphasises how forms of enveloping spatiality can "feel dangerous", how we *sense* something to be wrong. Conversely, security practices themselves increasingly seek to produce such affective atmospheres, generating a sense of comfort and protection.

How does the blurring discussed in this book involve intentional arrangements of bodies, objects and spaces that engender sensations of fear, or conversely safety? Atreyee Sen's discussion of the embodied geographies of fear hints at this, while Helene Maria Kyed's analysis of specific objects, such as uniforms and batons, suggests not only their symbolic power, but their ability to mobilise affect. More broadly, we might understand uncertainty – an effect of security's blurring that is emphasised in multiple chapters in this volume – not only as a cognitive state, one of not knowing, but also as an affective one. The lack of clarity that marks many of the security performances the authors discuss can generate atmospherically immersive sensations, that to some may feel like safety, and to others like danger.

This brings me to a last point, one that is more political than conceptual per se. This book takes an explicitly critical perspective on blurring. Across contexts, we see how the lack of clarity surrounding the boundaries between security providers, their agents and their goals enables discrimination and exclusion. In some cases, this is a state-sanctioned differentiation of citizenship, in others it emerges from acts of self-help security that are actively pursued by marginalised populations. As academics, critique may be what we do best. We are not necessarily obligated, nor always well-positioned, to formulate solutions to complex problems. Yet this book raises important questions about how to deal with security blurs – will insisting on more clarity enhance more just and democratic political relations? Is exclusion inherent to any type of security act, and does blurring aggravate this? Or does a certain level of fuzziness in terms of boundaries also allow disenfranchised groups and individuals more room for manoeuvre in their relations with the state and other governance actors? Like security itself, the question of how to act on, or intervene in, security blurs remains surrounded by uncertainty.

References

Adey, Peter. 2014. "Security Atmospheres or the Crystallisation of Worlds". *Environment and Planning D: Society and Space* 32 (5): 834–851.

Anderson, Ben. 2009. "Affective Atmospheres". *Emotion, Space and Society* 2 (2): 77–81.

Arias, Enrique Desmond, and Daniel M. Goldstein, eds. 2010. *Violent Democracies in Latin America*. Durham: Duke University Press.

Boudreau, Julie-Anne, and Diane E. Davis. 2017. "Introduction: A Processual Approach to Informalization". *Current Sociology* 65 (2): 151–166.

Frossard, Carolina, and Rivke Jaffe. 2018. "Security and Technology". In *Routledge Handbook of Anthropology and the City: Engaging the Urban and the Future*, edited by Setha Low, 117–128. London: Routledge.

Koster, Martijn. 2014. "Brazilian Brokers, Boundaries and Buildings: A Material Culture of Politics". *Journal of Material Culture* 19 (2): 125–144.

Star, Susan Leigh, and James R. Griesemer. 1989. "Institutional Ecology, Translations and Boundary Objects: Amateurs and Professionals in Berkeley's Museum of Vertebrate Zoology, 1907–39". *Social Studies of Science* 19 (3): 387–420.

Smart, Alan. 2012. "Anthropological Shades of Grey: Informal Norms and Becoming (il)legal". *Keynote Presented at Conference "Norms in the Margin and Margins of the Norm. The Social Construction of Illegality"*, Royal Museum of Central Africa, October 25–27. https://prism.ucalgary.ca/bitstream/handle/1880/52156/Anthropological_shades_of_grey_PLAIN%20TEXT.pdf?sequence=6.

Index

Note: Page numbers in **bold** indicate a table and page numbers in *italics* indicate a figure on the corresponding page.